Cambridge Elements

Elements in Language Teaching
edited by
Heath Rose
University of Oxford
Jim McKinley
University College London

LANGUAGE TEACHER EMOTIONS

Juyoung Song
Murray State University

Elizabeth R. Miller
University of North Carolina at Charlotte

Shaftesbury Road, Cambridge CB2 8EA, United Kingdom

One Liberty Plaza, 20th Floor, New York, NY 10006, USA

477 Williamstown Road, Port Melbourne, VIC 3207, Australia

314–321, 3rd Floor, Plot 3, Splendor Forum, Jasola District Centre, New Delhi – 110025, India

103 Penang Road, #05–06/07, Visioncrest Commercial, Singapore 238467

Cambridge University Press is part of Cambridge University Press & Assessment, a department of the University of Cambridge.

We share the University's mission to contribute to society through the pursuit of education, learning and research at the highest international levels of excellence.

www.cambridge.org
Information on this title: www.cambridge.org/9781009594158

DOI: 10.1017/9781009594134

© Juyoung Song and Elizabeth R. Miller 2025

This publication is in copyright. Subject to statutory exception and to the provisions of relevant collective licensing agreements, no reproduction of any part may take place without the written permission of Cambridge University Press & Assessment.

When citing this work, please include a reference to the DOI 10.1017/9781009594134

First published 2025

A catalogue record for this publication is available from the British Library

ISBN 978-1-009-59415-8 Hardback
ISBN 978-1-009-59414-1 Paperback
ISSN 2632-4415 (online)
ISSN 2632-4407 (print)

Cambridge University Press & Assessment has no responsibility for the persistence or accuracy of URLs for external or third-party internet websites referred to in this publication and does not guarantee that any content on such websites is, or will remain, accurate or appropriate.

For EU product safety concerns, contact us at Calle de José Abascal, 56, 1°, 28003 Madrid, Spain, or email eugpsr@cambridge.org

Language Teacher Emotions

Elements in Language Teaching

DOI: 10.1017/9781009594134
First published online: September 2025

Juyoung Song
Murray State University

Elizabeth R. Miller
University of North Carolina at Charlotte

Author for correspondence: Juyoung Song, jsong2@murraystate.edu

Abstract: This Element provides readers with an overview of major approaches, concepts, and research on language teacher emotions (LTE) along with related pedagogical approaches. It begins by situating LTE within the context of the affective turn in language education. The discussion then moves through psycho-cognitive approaches, followed by critical approaches on LTE, highlighting key concepts and research contributions within each framework. The Element next explores pedagogical approaches to LTE, offering practices that can be used in teacher education programs alongside a set of reflective questions that foster critical inquiry on emotions among language teachers. Finally, it addresses ethical concerns and outlines future directions for LTE research.

Keywords: language teachers, emotions, wellbeing, identity, teacher education

© Juyoung Song and Elizabeth R. Miller 2025

ISBNs: 9781009594158 (HB), 9781009594141 (PB), 9781009594134 (OC)
ISSNs: 2632-4415 (online), 2632-4407 (print)

Contents

1 Language Teacher Emotions and the Affective Turn   1

2 Psycho-cognitive Approaches to Emotions   6

3 Critical Approaches to Emotions   23

4 Pedagogical Approaches   40

5 Ethical Considerations and Future Directions   53

   References   61

1 Language Teacher Emotions and the Affective Turn

Emotions are a dynamic and integral part of teachers' work, and all institutions, particularly schools, are filled with emotions. For that reason, it is clear that teaching needs to be understood as fundamentally an emotional practice (Hargreaves, 1998). However, attention to emotion in language teacher education has only recently begun to receive scholarly focus. The nature of language education, in particular, requires language teachers – perhaps more so than teachers in other fields – to facilitate highly interactive activities that foster student engagement, wellbeing, and empowerment. This, in turn, places additional pressure on language teachers and heightens their emotional burden, as they strive to inspire, support, and care for their students both inside and outside the classroom (Acheson et al., 2016; Gkonou & Miller, 2019, Morris, 2022; Smith & King, 2018; Song, 2022; Warner & Diao, 2022). Historically, however, emotions have been overlooked or excluded from language teacher education, as they have often been framed as obstacles to effective classroom practice and professional development. For example, language teacher anxiety has been widely researched and is often perceived as an indicator of incompetence or linguistic insecurity (Morris & King, 2024).

Over the last decade and a half, in line with the affective turn (Pavlenko, 2013) in Second Language Acquisition (SLA) research, language teacher emotions (LTE) have garnered significant scholarly attention (see reviews by Han et al., 2023; Morris & King, 2024; Tao et al., forthcoming; Yang & Sato, forthcoming). The rapid growth in LTE research suggests that the topic of teacher emotions has resonated deeply with language scholars and teachers alike, and many scholars agree that LTE research has now emerged as a field of study in its own right. Furthermore, this research has been undertaken by researchers who align with a range of theoretical perspectives. The increasing interest in LTE may stem, in part, from the cumulative and often emotionally demoralizing effects of school reforms that prioritize standardized testing over humanistic education, as well as the declining societal and institutional value placed on language learning. In recent years, the topic has taken on even greater relevance as the disruptive effects of the global pandemic on both teachers' and students' lives – specifically their emotional wellbeing – have been observed and experienced firsthand.

In this section, we first explore how the social and affective turns in second language acquisition research have contributed to the emergence of LTE research. Next, we introduce the goals and scope of this Element and outline its structure, offering a brief overview of each section.

1.1 Context for the Affective Turn and LTE Research

While LTE research is a relatively new phenomenon, the seeds for its development in SLA research were planted several decades ago. Historically, SLA research focused primarily on identifying the most effective language teaching methods and analyzing the factors or variables that lead to better student learning outcomes. The emphasis was on optimizing language learning processes, often through cognitive and linguistic perspectives, with less attention given to the personal, social, and emotional aspects of language education. The social turn in SLA research (Block, 2003), which began in the 1990s and expanded rapidly in the early 2000s, provided fertile ground for the affective turn (Pavlenko, 2013) by broadening the scope of language learning and teaching beyond individual cognitive processes and emphasizing the importance of social context, interaction, identity, and power relations (Block, 2007; Norton, 2000; Prior, 2019).

One noteworthy contribution to this social turn is Vygotskian theory (see the Element by Poehner & Lantolf, 2024), which posits that all learning, including language learning, is a socially and culturally mediated process that emerges through interactions with more knowledgeable others and with culturally significant artifacts (Vygotsky, 1978). As SLA researchers began to focus on the social and cultural aspects of language learning in the 1990s, they recognized that language acquisition could not be fully understood without considering learners' social environments or their "culture-specific interactions" (Lantolf, 2000, p. 79). This shift in focus also brought issues of identity and power dynamics to the forefront.

The growing attention to identity in SLA research and in the emerging field of language teacher research led to the recognition that identity is also deeply intertwined with emotional experiences (Golombek & Johnson, 2004). For instance, learners' and teachers' feelings of belonging, exclusion, confidence, or vulnerability are essential to understanding their negotiation of identity as part of the learning and teaching process (Song, 2016). Building on this focus on identity and interaction, SLA researchers began to explore the influence of emotion in language learners' experiences (Barcelos, 2015; Oxford, 2015) and on how emotions influence language teachers' professional identities (Benesch, 2012; Cowie, 2011) as well as their cognitive development (Golombek & Doran, 2014).

We can now say that LTE research has come to embrace the understanding that "emotions are at the heart of teaching" (Hargreaves, 1998, p. 835), an idea first introduced by general education researchers (Hargreaves, 1998; Zembylas, 2003). With the maturing of LTE research in recent years, we have learned that emotions are integral to understanding how teachers negotiate their roles, manage relationships with students, peers, and administrators, and cope with the challenges they face in their daily teaching practices. This LTE scholarship has highlighted the importance of teachers' emotion regulation, emotion(al) labor, emotion literacy, and emotional vulnerability, among many other topics that we explore in greater detail throughout this Element.

An overriding concern of LTE research, whether explicit or implicit, is the need to foster and maintain teacher wellbeing (MacIntyre et al., 2019). When language teachers are burned out, contending with job insecurity, and/or dealing with chronic stress, they tend to be less effective teachers and may even choose to leave their teaching careers. Furthermore, as scholars increasingly focus on the social and institutional contexts that often position language teachers in challenging and complex power hierarchies, they have identified the emotional toll these external factors take on language teachers. In this way, LTE research has underscored the importance of supporting teachers' emotional resilience, agency, and wellbeing.

1.2 The Goals and Scope of This Element

This Element offers a timely exploration of LTE from multiple perspectives, addressing the interaction of cognition, psychology, identity, and emotions in relation to social dynamics and power in language teachers' professional work and personal growth. We aim to provide an overview of two major theoretical frameworks, examining major differences between psycho-cognitive and critical approaches to LTE. In doing so, we introduce key concepts from each approach and discuss how relevant research has contributed to our understanding of language teachers' emotions, professional practices and identity.

Additionally, we seek to bridge LTE research and language teacher education by emphasizing the pedagogical implications of LTE. In presenting praxis-focused pedagogies, we introduce several teacher education practices that can promote critical inquiry into emotion, accompanied by an example set of reflective questions for language teachers.

We also attempt to strike a balance between scholarly discussion of LTE research and practical application to research practices by sharing our first-hand experiences. The LTE research that we have conducted has, in many ways, transformed how we engage with the emotions embedded in our own professional lives as well as the experiences of the teachers we have worked alongside. Therefore, each section of this Element integrates our experiences through personal narratives or dialogues between us, offering reflections alongside theoretical and research-based insights on LTE.

As the aim of this Element is not to provide a comprehensive review of LTE research* but rather to share our insights and perspectives on diverse approaches and research findings, we place particular emphasis on the theoretical approaches that we consider significant based on our professional experiences and interpretations. We are well aware of the ongoing variability in how scholars have classified the guiding theories for LTE research (Barcelos et al., 2022; Benesch, 2017; Yang & Sato, forthcoming; White, 2018). Barcelos et al. (2022), for example, classify biological, cognitive, and psychological theoretical frameworks all as psychological approaches, whereas Benesch (2017) discusses only cognitive approaches. Similar to Barcelos et al. (2022), we have elected to group LTE research that draws on cognitive and/or psychological theories under one theoretical umbrella, which we are calling the psycho-cognitive framework. In Section 2, we discuss some of the different conceptual foci adopted in this body of work but view the strength of their shared features as sufficient reason to combine them into the single, albeit broad, category. We also recognize that scholars often draw on more than one theoretical framework within the same study. As such, our classification into two theoretical orientations – psycho-cognitive and critical – may be better understood as representing two ends of a spectrum, with some concepts and theories positioned somewhere between these ends. For example, Vygotskian sociocultural theory focuses on individual cognition and psychology but also emphasizes social interaction and cultural mediation in showing how they all are inextricably interconnected in cognitive development (e.g. Golombek & Doran, 2014). Similarly, LTE research that aligns with an ecological perspective often relies on the quantitative tools and methods that typically are part of research following the psycho-cognitive traditions (Han et al., 2023). However, the same research also often focuses on the relationships between teacher

---

* For readers interested in the insights available from meta-analyses or scoping reviews of research on language teacher emotions, we urge you to consult the following recent and forthcoming publications. Han et al. (2023) report on the main research foci, research methods used, and theoretical approaches adopted in journal articles published between 2005 and 2022. Morris and King (2024) review journal articles published between 2010 and 2020 and provide an overview of the general findings and research methods used in these publications; Tao et al. (forthcoming) identify four main research themes that have emerged in LTE-focused journal articles published between 2015 and 2024 along with demographic information on where the research was conducted and with whom. Yang and Sato (forthcoming) provide a historical timeline that identifies the most influential studies on LTE, starting in 1996 and continuing through 2024. Each of these overviews offers useful insights that help readers understand how the LTE field of inquiry has developed over time. There is some overlap in terms of the time periods covered, with each covering some part of the 2010–2020 decade when LTE research began to accelerate. Because of the methods used to identify relevant publications, these overviews are only able to cover journal articles. For other useful resources, readers are encouraged to consult extant edited collections on LTE (de Dios Martínez Agudo, 2018; Feryok, 2024; Gkonou, Dewaele, King, 2020; Simons & Smits, 2020).

emotions, their identities, and institutional and sociopolitical factors that tend to be the concerns of critical research (Nazari et al., 2023). In acknowledging this variability in how LTE scholars theorize their work, we still maintain that the broad categories of psycho-cognitive and critical approaches provide a useful structure for organizing the research that we discuss throughout this Element.

1.3 Plan of the Element

In Section 2, we introduce psycho-cognitive approaches to LTE. To account for the diversity of emphases in this large body of research, we have chosen to introduce nine key concepts that are informed by psycho-cognitive theories. We then discuss the contributions of this LTE research by first examining how it has expanded our understanding of teacher cognition, knowledge, and beliefs and how it has served to validate teacher emotions. Next, we describe some of the practical strategies that have been proposed for language teachers in addressing or managing their emotional challenges. We also discuss how practices that support language teacher wellbeing can benefit students and often lead to further, indirect positive effects for teachers. We then discuss the implications of this research and offer suggestions for future work. This section includes a personal reflection by one of us, Elizabeth "Liz", on her early encounter with LTE research and its impact on her professional identity.

In Section 3, we discuss a number of theoretical influences that can broadly be defined as critical approaches to LTE and introduce six key concepts that have emerged from this scholarship. We then examine the historical, cultural, and ideological contexts of language teachers' emotional experiences, followed by an analysis of the interconnections between language teacher power, emotional expression, and agency. We next focus on the role of emotions in language teacher identity negotiation and development. Similar to Section 2, we discuss the implications of this research along with suggestions for future scholarship. This section also includes Juyoung's personal reflection on how she became interested in LTE research and how she has developed her scholarship while navigating vulnerability and ethical challenges.

In Section 4, we introduce critical pedagogies that place emotions at the center of their practice. These selected pedagogies promote language teachers' praxis by fostering critical inquiry into their own emotions. We then present pedagogical activities that have been implemented in language teacher education and LTE research, discussing their pedagogical potential. Following this, we offer a set of reflective questions designed to encourage language teachers to engage in critical reflection on their emotions. We conclude this section by addressing key considerations for implementing emotion-related pedagogies into language teacher education programs. Additionally, this section includes a dialogue between us on our reflections and experiences on pedagogies related to LTE.

In Section 5, we outline directions for advancing LTE research and relevant pedagogy from its current state. To promote further inquiry, we discuss the critical role of researcher reflexivity and highlight various ethical concerns that LTE researchers encounter and must address. We conclude the Element by proposing potential directions for future research.

2 Psycho-cognitive Approaches to Emotions

Research in SLA and its pedagogical applications have long been dominated by theories or frameworks based in scholars' understandings of cognitive and psychological processes that shape language learning. Interestingly, alongside the social turn in SLA (Block, 2003), which facilitated its more recent affective turn, there has been a rapid increase of LTE research by scholars who continue to draw on psycho-cognitive frameworks. In considering this recent LTE work, it is important to note that education scholars had begun to explore the interconnection of emotions and cognition in teacher knowledge as early as the 1970s (e.g. Scheffler, 1977). In fact, many of these scholars point back to John Dewey's (1895) argument for the unity of emotion and cognition in human action (e.g. Garrison, 2003). Recognition of emotion and cognition as intersecting and co-influencing forces surfaced much later in SLA research, and even into the 1990s, it still focused almost exclusively on language learners rather than teachers (e.g. Arnold & Brown, 1999; Oxford, 1995). However, by the early 2000s, attention began to shift toward exploring how emotions and cognition relate to language teacher knowledge and/or beliefs, sometimes through drawing on Vygotskian sociocultural theory (e.g. Golombek & Johnson, 2004).

When we move forward to the 2010s, the decade when LTE research began to gain momentum, and the 2020s when its growth surged, the boundary between what is considered cognitive and what is considered psychological research becomes increasingly fuzzy. In order to foreground these interlinked elements, we have coined the term psycho-cognitive approaches to categorize this body of research (see Section 1.2 for the details of our rationale).

These studies tend to focus on teacher emotions as individual, internal feelings, often relying on self-reports via surveys, questionnaires, and various emotion scales or inventories. Teacher emotions tend to be sorted into categories of negative or positive emotions, a priori, and are often treated as universal experiences across language teachers. Contextual influences on teacher emotions, when considered, are usually treated as dependent variables. Using quantitative methods, the preferred methodology in most psycho-cognitive LTE research, allows researchers to compare outcomes across large populations of teachers and sometimes across national cultures. This research frequently offers useful strategies for teachers to practice in order to enhance their emotional resilience. As will be shown in Section 3, many of these characteristics of LTE research contrast with research drawing on critical approaches to emotions. At the same time, we recognize that not all of the LTE research that we have classified as psycho-cognitive adopts the methodologies described earlier. For example, research that aligns with Vygotskian theory and the notion of perezhivanie typically uses only qualitative methodologies, such as interviews, reflection journals, and/or classroom observations, and often uses discourse analysis to interpret the data.

In the following section, we attempt to identify the fundamental cognitive and psychological underpinnings of the key concepts that are found in these psycho-cognitive studies.

2.1 Key Concepts

2.1.1 Appraisal

Appraisal or cognitive *re*appraisal occurs when individuals evaluate particular situations to determine whether they constitute a "threat, challenge or benefit" to their emotional wellbeing (Lazarus, 1991, p. 822). LTE researchers view teacher emotions as developing in response to teachers' interpretations or cognitive appraisals of classroom and other teaching-related situations. Appraisal theory was developed in the field of psychology (Lazarus, 1991) but differed from other psychological approaches to emotion, such as stimulus-response theories, in arguing that the same stimulus can trigger vastly different emotional responses in individuals and that these responses can change over time. Given this variation in emotional responses and their dynamic nature, appraisal theory argues that there must be an intervening cognitive evaluation of an event, between the time of the event and an individual's emotional response to it. That is, different individuals will cognitively appraise the same situation differently, resulting in varied individual emotional responses.

LTE research drawing on appraisal theory has tended to focus on discrete emotions that emerge as a result of individual teachers' cognitive evaluations of particular situations and are often combined with the psychological concept of emotion regulation (see Section 2.1.6). For example, Goetze (2023) explored language teachers' emotional responses to classroom scenarios, presented to them as researcher-developed vignettes, that were designed to be anxiety provoking. The results of her survey with 272 foreign language teachers found that their emotional responses to the sample vignettes varied greatly. In fact, emotional responses of "determination, optimism, and interest" occurred more frequently than did anxiety responses (p. 335). Goetze thus argues that appraisal theory provides a compelling theoretical framework to explain the complexity in language teachers' emotional lives. She also contends that as teachers learn about and reflect on how they appraise challenging situations, they can learn to regulate or control their emotional responses.

2.1.2 Positive Psychology

Positive psychology has emerged quite recently as a (sub)theory within the broader psychological framework influencing LTE research. Positive psychology (Seligman & Csikszentmihalyi, 2000) focuses on topics such as "flow, hope, courage, wellbeing, optimism, creativity, happiness, flourishing, grit, resilience, positive emotions" (Dewaele et al., 2019, p. 2) among many other "positive" topics. Strong proponents of positive psychology for LTE research, Dewaele et al. (2019) acknowledge that the traditional focus of psychological research on negative experiences, such as anxiety, burnout, frustration, or anger, is still important, but argue that it needs to be complemented by investigations into what contributes to language teacher flourishing.

Beyond the benefits of positive psychology for teachers in terms of their own wellbeing, Mercer et al. (2016) add that numerous studies have found a "causal connection between teacher well-being, student performance and quality of teaching" (p. 216). Much of the SLA research influenced by positive psychology continues to focus on how teachers can support language learners, but there is a growing emphasis on how to support language teachers' psychological wellbeing. One such example is Sulis et al.'s (2022) survey study of 472 language teachers located around the world. They found a strong correlation between teachers' positive emotions and their sense of hope, optimism, and ability to find meaning in their work. Their study also identified the role of physical health in promoting language teacher wellbeing.

2.1.3 Perezhivanie

Perezhivanie, a Russian word, is a component of Vygotsky's (1978) sociocultural theory, which understands human cognition to develop in social interaction with more knowledgeable others and through the mediating effects of cultural tools (such as language). Vygotskian scholars have found his concept of perezhivanie to be a powerful theoretical tool for understanding the contributing role of emotions to language teacher cognitive development and change. This borrowed Russian term does not translate easily into English. It has been described as a "dialectic unity" of intellect and emotion in human experience (Zhang et al., 2022, p. 3). Smirnova (2023, p. 178) describes it as the "unity of the emotional and intellectual sides of human beings" in which external social and cultural influences are merged with an "individual's thought processes" over time. Because of its emphasis on emotions in cognitive development, LTE research that draws on perezhivanie concepts tends to be conducted over a period of time. For example, Amory and Johnson (2023, p. 12) traced the psychological development of novice teachers as they contended with and made sense of, or "intellectualized," their emotional experiences while advancing through their pre-service teaching assignments. They found that as these teacher learners (TLs) intentionally brought "cognition-and-emotion" together, treating them as "interconnected" through careful reflection on their emotional experiences, they were able to transform how they conceptualized teaching and themselves as teachers (p. 12). Given its emphasis on social interaction and discourse, LTE research informed by Vygotskian sociocultural theory and focusing on perezhivanie does not fit easily into the psycho-cognitive paradigm that we discuss in this section; however, because of its emphasis on cognitive and psychological development as emerging from interaction and social mediation, we have elected to include the key concept of perezhivanie alongside other psycho-cognitive concepts.

2.1.4 Emotional Intelligence

Emotional intelligence is typically regarded as an individual competence or personality trait that enables language teachers to recognize emotional triggers in their teaching contexts and to regulate their emotions in those situations. A psychological construct, emotional intelligence is often researched through psychometric performance measures such as the Trait Emotional Intelligence Questionnaire (TEIQue) (Petrides, 2009), which measures the factors that are understood to form language teachers' emotional intelligence. Emotional intelligence research most frequently tries to determine if there are correlations between language teachers' levels of emotional intelligence and other constructs such as their self-efficacy (Nikoopour et al., 2012) or their involvement in reflective practices (Seydi Shahivand & Moradkhani, 2020), among many others.

While emotional intelligence is understood to be a component of personality, and thus is often referred to as a trait, researchers have also argued that it can be developed or enhanced over time and with accumulating experience (Gkonou & Mercer, 2017). The construct of emotional intelligence continues to interest scholars because language teachers identified as having high emotional intelligence are reported to be more successful in their work. They have, for example, been found to manage the challenges of classroom life more ably, hold more positive attitudes toward their students and their professional work, be more creative in the classroom, and have better relationships with students and colleagues (Dewaele et al., 2018).

2.1.5 Emotional Literacy

Emotional literacy is closely related to emotional intelligence and both terms are often used interchangeably. Language teachers with high emotional literacy are able to understand, express, and manage their emotions appropriately, a capacity which allows them to improve their own wellbeing and that of others. A key difference is that emotional literacy is usually regarded as a set of skills or strategies that can be developed rather than a personality trait (Kliueva & Tsagari, 2018). To date, emotional literacy has more frequently been explored in relation to how language teachers can enhance it among their students (Kliueva & Tsagari, 2018) than as a characteristic to be investigated among teachers. That said, very recent research has shown that increasing language teachers' emotional literacy can also increase their motivation, emotion regulation capacity, empathy toward their students, and capacity to interact with students and colleagues successfully (Rezai et al., 2024).

Despite the positioning of emotional literacy as a set of learned skills, Tao et al. (forthcoming) argue that the distinction between the malleability attributed to emotional literacy and the greater permanence assigned to emotional intelligence is still an open question and requires more attention. We have also observed that in many cases researchers refer to emotional literacy as a "catch-all" descriptor of teachers' capacity to manage their emotions effectively for a given context rather than a clear-cut researchable construct in its own right.

2.1.6 Emotion Regulation or Management

Emotion regulation or management refers to language teachers' capacity to control their emotional displays and even the emotions that they feel. While this concept, informed by psychological theories, overlaps with emotional intelligence and emotional literacy, emotion regulation gives emphasis to the strategies adopted by language teachers to control their own emotions and sometimes those of their students. These strategies are sometimes categorized as up-regulation and down regulation; up-regulation refers to strategies that increase one's positive emotional experiences and down-regulation to strategies which decrease negative emotions (Gross et al., 2006). Morris and King (2024) argue that because emotion regulation strategies can be learned, "reflective training sessions" (p. 19) should be offered to language teachers so that they can protect themselves more effectively from workplace stresses and learn how to control students' disruptive behaviors.

As with emotional intelligence and emotional literacy, emotion regulation is often examined in relation to other constructs (sometimes referred to as variables) such as teachers' psychological wellbeing (Greenier et al., 2021; Talbot & Mercer, 2018), frustrations arising from student behaviors and working conditions (Morris & King, 2018), and teacher burnout (Fathi et al., 2021; Shen, 2022). Skillful use of emotion regulation strategies has been found to enable language teachers to enjoy higher levels of wellbeing, be more engaged in their workplace and classrooms, and be more resilient in the face of frustrations and challenges (see Tao et al., forthcoming, for an overview).

2.1.7 Emotional Dissonance

Emotional dissonance refers to the incongruence between emotions that are genuinely experienced and emotions that are outwardly expressed in order to meet or conform to external expectations (King & Ng, 2018). Research on emotional dissonance demonstrates that it closely intersects with cognitive dissonance. That is, emotional dissonance arises when teachers experience contradictions between what they regard as ideal situations for their classrooms and what actually occurs (Kubaniyiova, 2012) or between the "ideal and the real" (Li & Zhang, 2023, p. 2). Teachers often experience such contradictions as psychological stress or anxiety (Martínez Agudo, 2024). Much of the LTE research on emotional dissonance draws on Vygotskian sociocultural theory, and given the unity of cognition and emotion in Vygotskian perspectives, it is not surprising that both cognitive and emotional dissonance are regarded as "inextricably intertwined" (Kim et al., 2023, p. 3). Despite the negative connotations of dissonance, LTE research demonstrates that cognitive and emotional dissonance are not always detrimental if they can be transformed into "growth points," particularly in the context of teacher education programs (Golombek & Doran, 2014; Kubaniyiova, 2012). At the same time, researchers have noted that emotional dissonance does not always lead to professional growth or conceptual change, even when teacher educators seek to mediate such change (Golombek & Doran, 2014; Kubaniyiova, 2012). While it is not surprising that pre-service teachers might need to contend with emotional and cognitive dissonance in learning to become language teachers, research has found that neither in-service teachers (Martínez Agudo, 2024) nor teacher educators (Golombek, 2015) are immune to emotional dissonance. That is, emotional dissonance can support the professional growth of TLs – both pre-service and in-service teachers – as well as teacher educators, when it leads to careful, critical self-reflection on their experiences of emotional dissonance.

A growing number of researchers have begun to focus on the impact of tensions in language teacher practice (Tajeddin & Yazan, 2024). Teachers' emotional tensions and emotional dissonance both arise in similar situations (Tajeddin & Keshvari, 2025); however, research on tensions typically focuses on language teacher identity development in relation to personal, interpersonal, institutional, and social tensions (Nazari et al., 2025; Ustuk & Yazan, 2023) rather than the cognitive/emotional pairing examined in emotional dissonance research.

2.1.8 Emotional Labor

Emotional labor refers to individuals' efforts to control their emotions so as to render them "appropriate" for their work contexts. Emotional labor is often used interchangeably with emotion regulation or emotion management in research drawing on psychological theories (e.g. Dewaele & Wu, 2021). It also connects to emotional dissonance in highlighting the distress that teachers can experience when their actual emotions do not match an idealized emotional self; however, emotional labor diverges from emotional dissonance in emphasizing the role that institutions play in setting the norms for "appropriate" emotions. The concept was developed by sociologist Arlie Hochschild (1983) to explain how and why many people find it necessary to manage and display their emotions in particular ways in order to meet the emotional requirements of their jobs and be regarded as effective employees. She used the term "surface acting" to describe employees' efforts to hide their authentic emotions and outwardly display or pretend to feel only those emotions deemed appropriate in their workplaces. "Deep acting" describes employees' mental efforts to actually feel the approved emotions. Hochschild linked these psychological concepts to institutional power hierarchies and gendered inequities, but these social and contextual aspects of emotional labor are more frequently adopted in research informed by critical theoretical frameworks and such efforts are usually referred to as "emotion labor" in those studies (see Section 3.1.1 for more discussion on emotion labor). In a study conducted with Chinese language teachers working in Cameroon, Hulda and Zhao (2024, p. 5) identified how practicing surface acting by smiling and "pretending that everything is fine," even when they felt angry or frustrated contributed to these teachers' emotional labor. However, their achievement of deep acting, that is, making an effort to express real empathy to their students, was not typically associated with emotional labor for them but corresponded with what they described as "naturally felt positive emotions" (p. 7). Hulda and Zhao contend that these teachers' efforts at both surface acting and deep acting were employed to align with Cameroonian sociocultural norms regarding the emotions that are deemed appropriate for teachers to feel and display in the classroom.

Research which adopts a psychological perspective to emotional labor often focuses on changes that language teachers can make in their classroom practice, strategies for avoiding situations that trigger negative emotions and for promoting those that lead to positive emotions, and/or changing their mental perceptions (i.e. through cognitive reappraisal) of their professional experiences (Ghanizadeh & Royaei, 2015; King & Ng, 2018).

2.1.9 Wellbeing

Wellbeing is an expansive psychological construct that incorporates a broad array of factors that contribute to language teacher flourishing. Informed by positive psychology (see Section 2.1.2) research on language teacher wellbeing aims to support teacher happiness, satisfaction, creativity, resilience, satisfaction, sense of accomplishment or self-efficacy, and their ability to find meaning in their work. Many researchers distinguish between hedonic or eudaimonic perspectives of wellbeing in which the former refers to individuals' subjective experience of happiness, pleasure, and other desirable emotions while the latter refers to individuals' experience of finding meaning, fulfillment, and self-actualization (Mercer, 2023; Mercer & Murillo-Miranda, 2025). These varied components show that wellbeing is not just about feeling good but is more focused on teachers' capacity to thrive in their professional roles (MacIntyre et al., 2019). For that reason, researchers are interested in determining the stressors that can thwart language teacher wellbeing and the practices that promote it. Researchers have found that language teacher wellbeing directly affects student enjoyment and learning success (Dewaele et al., 2019; Zhang, 2021).

Although much of this psychologically oriented research remains focused on the internal feelings and perceptions of individual teachers, scholars have begun to pay more attention to the complex ecologies within which teacher wellbeing can be supported, arguing that "wellbeing does not reside solely within individuals but is socially situated too" (Mercer, 2021, p. 15). This expanded perspective asks that researchers consider the need for "systemic change and structural support" (p. 16) in institutions and asserts that responsibility for teacher wellbeing lies with institutions just as much as with individual teachers. We look forward to seeing more research account for the structural and institutional influences on teacher wellbeing.

In Box 1, Liz reflects on her experiences researching LTE including the concept of wellbeing.

Box 1 Liz's personal reflection on researching LTE

My entry into LTE research happened quite by accident. In 2015, my friend and colleague, Dr. Christina Gkonou, invited me to collaborate with her in analyzing a set of interviews that she had conducted with English teachers working in private language schools in Greece (see Gkonou & Miller, 2019). They were part of her larger study that focused on language learner anxiety. In her interviews with these teachers, Christina asked them to talk about how they understood their role in working with highly anxious students. She and I started out with a simple research question: What strategies do EFL teachers use to help their learners mitigate their anxiety?

I brought "fresh eyes" to the collaboration since I had not participated in planning or implementing this study. I also had never researched learner anxiety nor worked with language teachers prior to this invitation. As I began to read through the interview transcripts multiple times, what became evident to me, and then to Christina too, was these language teachers' own emotionality. In talking about how they worked to alleviate students' language learning anxiety, they also talked about their efforts to demonstrate care and be responsive to their students' needs. They indicated that these efforts to be caring were often accompanied by the rewards of seeing their students' language learning improvements, but they also used words like "worry" and "pressure," and provided examples of days when they did not feel "calm enough" to provide caring to students even when they believed that they should. We came to recognize that these teachers' efforts to be caring were examples of emotional labor, work which "involves many emotional costs, and is often invisible, unacknowledged, or devalued" (Isenbarger & Zembylas, 2006, p. 123), and that "it is often difficult to tell caring and emotional labour apart" (p. 133). It is something of an understatement to say that I found the scholarly work on emotional labor by Isenbarger and Zembylas (2006), among many other scholars, to be enlightening. I might even venture that it was personally transformative.

At the time that Christina and I were analyzing these interviews and reading the scholarly literature on teacher caring and emotional labor, I had been teaching for more than twenty years. This included two years as a high school English language arts teacher in Puerto Rico, a year and a half teaching EFL in Japan, a number of years as a teaching assistant and/or adjunct instructor of writing and ESL in university settings in the U.S., as well as nine years as a tenure-track university professor in a Department

Box 1 (cont.)

of English at my current university. Up until then, I had considered my anxieties, frustrations, vulnerabilities, along with feelings of satisfaction, pride, and even joy that accompanied my teaching, as highly personal – not something that I would typically talk about with peers and certainly not something that I would consider worthy of research. Encountering terms like emotion(al) labor, emotion management, and "discourses of affect" (Pavlenko, 2013, p. 18) suddenly gave new gravitas to my "personal" feelings. The new perspective on teacher emotions introduced in this scholarship was also liberating. I realized that my experiences with frustration and feelings of vulnerability did not need to be a source of shame, and that they were, in fact, normal for individuals working in publish-or-perish neoliberal universities who were also trying to build supportive relationships with and for students. I also was convinced that more teachers, particularly language teachers, needed to know about these ideas and that applied linguistics researchers needed to gain a clearer understanding of teachers' emotions and their effects.

My work with Christina in collaborative reading, analyzing, and writing about the accounts produced by the English teachers in Greece spurred us to undertake our own interview study focusing directly on language teachers' emotional experiences, first with teachers of English in the U.S. and the U.K. (Miller & Gkonou, 2018) and then with teachers of English in Germany and of Norwegian in Norway (Miller & Gkonou, 2023, 2024). In the interviews, teachers talked about situations that gave them great pride, made them happy, made them angry, or left them feeling overwhelmed at times. They talked about challenging working conditions, heavy workloads, and wonderfully supportive colleagues. They also described strategies they had developed for themselves to manage their emotions and those of their students.

While I learned an enormous amount from these teachers, who were so generous with their time, I also sensed that the interview encounters may have been beneficial for the teachers too. Like me, several commented that they had never considered teacher emotions as something worthy of research, and a number of them told me that they agreed to the interviews because they were intrigued by the topic. We always let them know that they could choose what they wanted to disclose and the degree of personal detail that they wanted to share, and I am certain that they had many more stories they could have told but perhaps were not willing to disclose. That said, it seemed to me that by asking them to talk about their emotional

> **Box 1 (cont.)**
>
> experiences, at least some of the teachers saw their emotions as validated, as important. For example, at the end of one interview, a teacher commented, "I think it's a really interesting area of study because it seems we are so often asked to think of the [teaching] methodology and sometimes forget we're people." I very much hope that all of the teachers found some personal benefit in participating in the interviews.
>
> As LTE research continues to proliferate, it seems clear that it addresses a topic that "feels" important to scholars and teachers, both personally and academically, just as it did for me. However, I am also aware that it is always fraught work. Asking teachers to talk about their emotions can feel intrusive and bring uncomfortable vulnerabilities to the surface that they may not want to make public. Even if I as a researcher want to understand the full scope of teacher emotions, I might never be able to access all of it. I think an important position that I (and other LTE researchers) need to adopt is that of intellectual humility – we can't know everything and we can't expect language teachers to divulge uncomfortable stories even when we think they might be useful to the field or for the individual teacher. In consideration of this tension, I've started a new project in which I have asked language program administers to talk about how they understand language teacher belonging and how they nurture belonging. While it is always important to hear from teachers themselves, I believe that it is also important to bring to light how their supervisors and/or other administrators with greater institutional power work to support the emotional lives of the teachers in their programs.

2.2 Contributions of the Research

2.2.1 Understanding the Intersection of Emotions with Cognition, Knowledge, and Beliefs

In recognizing the "pervasive emotional content" (Golombek & Doran, 2014, p. 102) that permeates teachers' cognitive development, we find that LTE research drawing on psycho-cognitive frameworks has, in turn, expanded and complexified our understanding of what language teacher cognition, knowledge, and beliefs entail (Burns et al., 2015; Xu, 2024). We view this expansion in our understanding of teacher cognition to be a particularly impactful outcome of psycho-cognitive research. As an example, Golombek and Doran's (2014) study, which draws on Vygotsky's notion of *perezhivanie,* examines a language teacher educator's written responses to a TL's emotionalized accounts of classroom experiences in a weekly reflection journal. They demonstrate how the teacher educators' responses helped to mediate that TL's cognitive development over the course of a term. In arguing for a unity of cognition and emotion, they indicate how the emotional content of the focal TL's journal entries "indexes areas where further cognitive/conceptual development may be needed to resolve emotional and cognitive dissonance," and that through mediating this resolution, the teacher educator engendered "a kind of feeling-for thinking" (p. 110).

Golombek and Doran (2014) also posit that by normalizing and validating TLs' emotions and treating them as "growth point[s]" and "valuable resource[s]" (p. 110), rather than moments of weakness, teacher educators can more effectively contribute to cognitive growth in novice teachers. In this way, Golombek and Doran's perspective supports Swain's (2013, p. 205) argument that "emotional and cognitive resources" both mediate learning," and that to ignore emotions leaves scholars with an incomplete understanding of cognitive development.

Relatedly, Yuan and Lee's (2014) study has shown that TLs can advance their cognitive learning apart from direct mediation from teacher educators. They found that as TLs reflected on new, and often challenging, emotional experiences in their practicum teaching, they often made adaptations to their pedagogical practice. Undertaking these changes enhanced these novice teachers' "confidence and motivation" (p. 487), and, just as important, Yuan and Lee conclude that TLs' intentional reflection on their emotions, along with ongoing classroom-based practice, helped them "build[] their capacity to engage in cognitive learning and construct their own knowledge" (p. 489). Given these positive outcomes, they recommend that teacher educators facilitate the potential for such cognitive learning by incorporating reflection on emotions into their teacher training courses.

The expansion in our understanding of language teacher cognition through incorporating teacher emotions holds true for our understanding of teacher beliefs as well. Language teacher beliefs, long regarded as cognitive constructs and a component of teacher knowledge, have been shown to be inextricable from teacher emotions. In the past decade and a half, researchers have begun to focus on the role that beliefs play in mediating teacher emotions and vice versa (Barcelos & Kalaja, 2011; Mercer, 2011). Drawing on Rodrigues' (2015) study with English TLs in Brazil, Barcelos and Ruohotie-Lyhty (2018) show how emotions shape beliefs. The study found that these TLs experienced negative emotions in relation to their inability to master English fully, quickly, and easily. However, these negative experiences sometimes resulted in a helpful change in their beliefs. That is, their belief that good English teachers had to have a high proficiency in the language changed to a belief that a good English teacher does not need to know everything about the language. Likewise, the positive emotions they experienced by some in relation to learning English led them to believe that good English teachers should "feel excited, engaged and attempt to make learning fun" (p. 117).

Barcelos and Ruohotie-Lyhty (2018) thus contend that both "positive and negative emotional experiences helped teacher [learners] to form new beliefs" (p. 117). Given the reciprocal influences of emotion and beliefs, Barcelos and Ruohotie-Lyhty (2023) recommend that language educators call attention to TLs' individually held beliefs about teaching and reflect on how those beliefs are informed by socioculturally informed understandings of good teaching as well as how they connect to their emotional experiences.

Many of the research studies discussed in this section support the notion that reflecting on emotions in teacher education or in professional development contexts can provide language teachers with opportunities for cognitive learning and for changing unhelpful or self-sabotaging beliefs about teaching. Such reflection and mindfulness in relation to emotions is relevant for language teachers at any stage in their career trajectory and can be undertaken on one's own, under the mentorship of teacher educators, or in community with one's peers. In this way, we see how a focus on teacher emotions, beliefs, and cognition together does more than advance researcher knowledge; it can also directly assist teachers in becoming more effective language teachers.

Perhaps of more immediate impact for language teachers is the understanding that their emotional experiences are important. If emotions are integral to teacher cognition, knowledge, and beliefs, then they are worthy of being researched and understood. In turn, teachers' individual, subjective emotional experiences are validated rather than sidelined as a distraction to "scientific" and "rational" research (cf. Golombek & Doran, 2014; Swain, 2013).

2.2.2 Promoting Language Teacher Emotional Wellbeing

Another important contribution of research drawing on psycho-cognitive approaches has been its ability to connect particular teacher attributes, strategies, and actions to enhanced teacher wellbeing. As an example, Xiyun et al. (2022) found that English teachers in Iran who demonstrated a stronger sense of self-efficacy in relation to the positive impact of their teaching on student learning experienced a higher level of wellbeing. Likewise, teachers who were more adept in practicing emotion regulation reported higher wellbeing. They thus recommended that teacher educators should help TLs learn to recognize how stressors influence their emotions and how they can practice emotion regulation. They likewise recommended that language program administrators create positive, open learning environments which can empower in-service teachers to reflect on and talk about their emotions, and provide development opportunities so that teachers can enhance their professional knowledge, which, in turn, can increase their self-efficacy. In this way, Xiyun et al. highlight the need for teachers at all stages of their careers to reflect on how they "manage and direct their emotions" (p. 8).

While many studies such as Xiyun et al.'s (2022) point to the implications of their findings for teacher training (see also Gkonou & Miller, 2023; Goetze, 2023; Khajavy et al., 2018), a number have identified and promoted very particular strategies or actions that language teachers can practice on their own (e.g. Frenzel et al., 2021; Heydarnejad et al., 2021). One of these, a study by Kliueva and Tsagari (2018), examined the teaching strategies adopted by teachers with high emotional intelligence. They found that these teachers were more likely to emotionally engage students, use humor, or use positive language. Likewise, they were more likely to show personal interest in students and be empathetic. In relation to student misbehavior, emotionally intelligent teachers were far less likely to take the misbehavior personally and were far more likely to try to find reasons behind the misbehavior and work to re-establish positive relationships with misbehaving students. They were also more likely to practice strategies that support students' emotional growth such as by helping them develop a sense of personal responsibility and learn to talk about their emotions.

Beyond identifying particular strategies practiced by emotionally intelligent teachers, Kliuva and Tsagari's (2018) study offers an encouraging note even for teachers who might not view themselves as gifted with high emotional intelligence. In fact, all of the teachers in their study practiced all of the selected teaching strategies. The difference lay in how frequently they were practiced. They found that teachers who rated high in emotional intelligence practiced the strategies described earlier more frequently than teachers with lower emotional intelligence ratings. With training and mentoring, it thus seems possible for all teachers to cultivate their emotional intelligence or emotional literacy to some degree (Gkonou & Mercer, 2017; Morris & King, 2024).

King and Ng's (2018) study offers a different set of practical strategies that teachers can adopt to improve their emotional wellbeing, what they refer to as preventative emotion regulation strategies. That is, rather than merely helping teachers know how to respond to emotional challenges, these strategies can help teachers prevent many emotionally difficult situations from emerging. The first strategy involves *modifying situations* or planning lessons and learning tasks that will incite positive student behaviors and avert those that can trigger negative emotional responses by teachers. The second, *deploying attention*, involves the teacher focusing on students' positive behaviors and ignoring problematic ones (if they are minor). The final strategy, *cognitive change*, asks teachers to learn to reappraise difficult situations through self-talk or reflection so that its triggering effects on them are lessoned. An example of such a situation is when a teacher learns to reappraise student silence as a signal of their anxiety rather than as a personal slight to the teacher. In addition to the two studies discussed here, one can find many others that identify practical strategies for teachers to adopt in dealing with challenging situations and in working to enhance their sense of wellbeing (e.g. MacIntyre et al., 2020; Mystkowska-Wiertelak, 2022; Talbot & Mercer, 2018).

2.2.3 Acknowledging the Relationship between Emotion and Professional Practices

Yet another contribution of LTE research based in psycho-cognitive approaches has been its demonstration of how practices that support language teacher wellbeing often have cascading positive effects. We believe that centering language teacher wellbeing is reason enough for research to recommend strategies and actions that teachers can adopt; however, the positive implications of these actions for student learning is also noteworthy. Aligning with a positive psychology framework, several LTE studies have found a correlation between higher levels of student enjoyment in the language classroom, the feeling of being supported by their teachers, and having teachers who engage easily with students (Dewaele et al., 2018; Jin & Dewaele, 2018; Li et al., 2018). For example, Moskowitz and Dewaele (2019) found that when language learners perceived that their teachers were satisfied in their chosen profession, the students' expressed more positive attitudes to language learning and higher motivation to learn. The authors surmised that teacher satisfaction is likely demonstrated through higher levels of engagement with students and an ability to create a supportive emotional atmosphere in the classroom. Relatedly, other research has identified connections between language teacher emotion regulation and increased student engagement (Morris, 2025; Morris & King, 2020, 2023; Pinner, 2019). At the same time, it is important to acknowledge that research has also found that the perceptions of students and teachers regarding the effectiveness of teachers' emotion regulation efforts can differ greatly (e.g. Bielak & Mystkowska-Wierelak, 2022).

Of course, one benefit of more successful and engaged students is that teachers come to view themselves as more effective in the classroom, which often leads them to feel that their relationships with students and peers are more rewarding. Such perceptions feed into teachers' heightened sense of wellbeing. It seems that what is emotionally beneficial for students is often emotionally beneficial for teachers too. It is also important to recognize that teachers can over-commit to caring for their students along with working to meet institutional and curricular standards in their attempts to be supportive, effective teachers. Because they believe that they should be caring, they may present themselves as caring and congenial even when they are feeling frustrated and stressed. In such cases, teachers' emotional labor can lead to even more frustration and stress (Gkonou & Miller, 2019; King & Ng, 2018; Miller & Gkonou, 2018).

For this reason, we support the recommendation of many of the scholars cited in this section who call for teacher training programs to overtly address TLs' emotions as they are learning how to become teachers. We also believe that developing peer support groups or organizing professional development workshops can be enormously beneficial for in-service language teachers, with the caveat that they focus on both validating teacher emotions as well as using that emotional energy to collectively work toward improving aspects of their professional work and institutional positionality. There is strength in numbers, after all.

Unfortunately, there is still very limited research that shows how to create teacher education or professional development programs that promote teacher wellbeing. Eraldemir-Tuyan's (2019) study is one of the few to offer a template for a training program developed to improve language teachers' emotional literacy. Eraldemir-Tuyan reports on a pilot program conducted with seventeen English teachers working in Türkiye who met once a week for three hours over a ten-week period. The researcher describes the six "cycles" adopted in the training program and lists the activities followed in each cycle. These include completing an Emotional Intelligence map among other diagnostic tools, reading relevant articles on emotional intelligence, writing learning logs, engaging in peer and whole-group discussion, conducting individual reflections, and participating in activities to practice the ideas under discussion. We hope to see more research studies such as Eraldemir-Tuyan's in the near future that provide guidelines for developing training programs and that report on their outcomes.

2.2.4 Implications and Suggestions

In thinking about some of the assumptions embedded in studies that align with psycho-cognitive frameworks, we see that they often put forward the understanding that emotions can be straightforwardly identified as positive or negative. While it may seem obvious that frustration and anger are negative emotions that should be controlled or mitigated and that satisfaction and happiness are positive emotions that should be amplified for teachers, we would like to propose that such dichotomous assumptions are not particularly helpful. For example, Rodrigues' (2015) study demonstrated that both positive and negative emotional experiences led TLs to form new beliefs about teaching. In discussing Rodrigues' work, Barcelos and Ruohotie-Lyhty (2018) demonstrated that so-called negative emotions provoked opportunities for TLs not only to change their beliefs but also to re-conceptualize challenging situations, transform some of their teaching practices, and develop better relationships with students and peers. Likewise, Richards (2022) points out that negative emotional experiences can prompt language teachers to pursue professional development opportunities. As Gao et al. (2024, p. 3) comment, there often seems to be a "positive role of negative emotions," which leads us to question the a priori dichotomy into negative and positive emotions.

Replacing the positive/negative binary with new ones, that is, desirable/undesirable, helpful/detrimental, constructive/destructive, will likely only preserve decontextualized assumptions that some emotions are good and some are not. We thus argue that researchers should explore what emotions actually do and how they function for teachers before making assessments of them as necessarily negative or positive. As research from the critical paradigm has demonstrated, mitigating so-called negative emotions (Benesch, 2020) or pursuing so-called positive emotions (Miller & Gkonou, 2023) may actually reinforce existing norms and power relations.

Another assumption that seems embedded in this research is that the unit of analysis should be the individual teacher. These studies typically rely on self-report surveys or questionnaires and/or interviews completed by individual teachers. On the one hand, this approach is quite logical given that researchers are looking for information that only individual language teachers are privy to – their own emotional experiences. Furthermore, the quantitative methods adopted in many of these studies, including the use of a range of psychometric instruments, allow for comparisons across large numbers of participants (e.g. Dewaele et al., 2018; Dewale & Wu, 2021) and for establishing correlations among a large number of variables (Frenzel et al., 2016). These methods serve to control, to some degree, the messy reality of teacher emotions. That said, there is also much that such methods miss. By controlling their messiness and focusing primarily on individual emotional experiences, these research approaches fail to account for the very powerful institutional, social, and ideological elements of language teachers' (and learners') emotionality (Benesch, 2017; Imai, 2010; Song & Park, 2019) as will be discussed in Section 3.

One can find evidence of some positive changes or expansions in how this research conceptualizes emotions, particularly in work focusing on language teacher wellbeing. Mercer (2023, p. 1056) argues in her study with language teachers working at private language schools based in Malta, that "wellbeing is not only subjective and individual, but it is also objective and social." She cites La Placa et al. (2013, p. 118) who understand wellbeing to include the "interplay between [teachers'] circumstances, locality, activities and psychological resources, including interpersonal relations" (cited in Mercer, 2023, p. 1056). For this reason, Mercer adopts an ecological approach to teacher wellbeing. Other studies adopting an ecological perspective to LTE have examined how gender ideologies and low social status (Nazari et al., 2023), traditional cultural values and curriculum reforms (Zhang & Yusof, 2024), limited international collaborations (Nazari & De Costa, 2024) and nationalism and neoliberal globalization (Li & De Costa, 2023) are all implicated in language teacher emotions.

Such studies are expanding how language teacher emotions are conceived, through incorporating these extra-individual factors. They typically draw on interview research though a growing number make use of classroom observations, reflective journals, and/or narrative frames as well. There are also a growing number of studies that have adopted a mix of quantitative tools such as surveys or questionnaires, along with qualitative tools such as interviews. These studies have demonstrated that the "external" factors intertwined in teacher emotions, including cultural values, ideologies, and sociopolitical contexts, are more complex than simple variables. In many cases, researchers cannot know in advance what these contributing elements are.

For this reason, we hope to see more LTE research incorporate ecological perspectives into their psycho-cognitive frameworks. We also see a need for more longitudinal research if we are to gain a clearer understanding of how emotions, contexts, and social ideologies are interconnected and how they shift in their interrelatedness over time. We recognize that this kind of research is more difficult and costly to undertake than cross-sectional designs but believe that it is necessary to advance the field of LTE research. As noted earlier, we also look forward to learning from training programs that have been intentionally organized around LTE. Such work can build on the studies that have helped us understand the importance of teacher emotions while actively striving to support teachers' wellbeing.

3 Critical Approaches to Emotions

Critical research shifts the focus from emotions as individual and internal experiences to the influence of social structures and power relations in constituting LTE.

For example, rather than targeting whether particular emotions have a positive or negative effect on language teachers, researchers pay attention to how institutional practices, ideological values, and/or unequal power positions in particular contexts provoke certain emotional responses in language teachers (e.g. Benesch, 2012, 2017; Her & De Costa, 2022). What might be regarded as a "negative" emotion, such as teacher frustration or anger, can, from a critical theoretical perspective, be interpreted as a "signal" that structures, practices and existing power relations need to be changed (Benesch, 2020).

Much of the LTE research that we describe as informed by critical theory adopts discursive and poststructural approaches to emotions (Benesch, 2017). While the role of power relations remains a defining feature, a poststructural approach regards emotions as discourses that circulate in schools and other social contexts. Poststructural researchers focus on how institutional structures, power relations, and dominant ideologies constitute the emotional experiences of language teachers. They investigate how those social factors determine which emotions are regarded as "appropriate" in a given situation and which should be suppressed or hidden; that is, it is "appropriate" for teachers to feel upset when students plagiarize rather than be sympathetic toward them and take into consideration the situations that motivate them to plagiarize (Benesch, 2017) or for "good" teachers to feel and show caring toward their students even when they are exhausted and overworked in order to ensure that their students will perform well on standardized tests (Pereira, 2018). The focus of research drawing on critical approaches is on understanding inequitable situations and dominant discourses that constitute LTE rather than on individual teachers' internal psychologies. Likewise, it promotes teachers' awareness of unequal teaching conditions and urges them to advocate for changes that support their work and wellbeing rather than simply emphasizing how they can better manage their emotions (Benesch & Prior, 2023).

3.1 Key Concepts

3.1.1 Emotion Labor

As discussed in Section 2.1.8, emotion labor refers to language teachers' efforts to align the emotions that they experience in their professional lives with the normalized expectations and institutional norms (for a detailed discussion on these norms, see Section 3.1.2 Feeling Rules) of their workplaces. This concept was first developed by sociologist Arlie Hochschild (1979, 1983) and has since been adopted by researchers investigating a wide range of workplaces, including those of language teachers (Benesch 2012, 2017). While emotion regulation or management (see Section 2.1.6), the psychological practice of controlling one's emotions and emotional expression, is practiced by all individuals to varying degrees in their personal lives as well as in more public contexts, Hochschild's concept is particular to workplaces, where managing emotions is important for earning a wage. Employees often feel compelled to bring their emotions in line with what is regarded as "appropriate" for their workplace in order to keep their jobs or be regarded as a valued employee.

It is important to understand a distinction in terminology. Hochschild referred to this work as *emotional* labor which included the psychological concepts of deep acting and surface acting, as described in 2.2.8. Benesch (2017) elected to use the term *emotion* labor to distinguish her poststructural, discursive orientation to LTE. Benesch wanted to avoid the negative connotations often associated with the term "emotional," a word which she notes is often associated with "overwrought" and undesirable emotional expressions and is often connected to women's emotions (p. 12). She also wanted to foreground the feminist and critical roots in the conceptualization of emotion labor that emphasize the centrality of power relations in both generating particular emotions and creating expectations for how they are best "managed" according to relevant feeling rules. Research on emotion labor thus centers power relations and institutional norms in understanding emotions and how they are "managed"; it also often uncovers how emotion labor leads to much greater benefits for the more powerful stakeholders in an organization. For example, when language teachers express caring in their classrooms, even when contending with challenging situations, their institutions greatly benefit when no one challenges unjust policies and practices, when teachers keep students (and their parents) happy, or when teacher employees undertake heavy workloads, often for low pay, and thus keep institutions financially viable (Pereira, 2018). This critically informed approach to emotion labor moves emotions out of individual psychology to how emotion discourses help to maintain unequal power (Benesch & Prior, 2023). Given its implications for power imbalances in teachers' experiences of emotion labor, emotion can become a space for resistance and self-transformation, enabling agency (Benesch, 2018) when teachers, through reflexivity, recognize their emotions and their relationship to the broader social context (see Section 3.1.5).

Emotion labor has been a prominent focus of LTE research, with numerous studies exploring language teachers' emotion labor in relation to teachers' sociocultural backgrounds, educational policies, assessment practices, online teaching, and English-medium instruction (EMI) (e.g. Gkonou & Miller, 2019; Kocabaş-Gedik & Ortaçtepe Hart, 2021; Nazari & De Costa, 2024; Nazari & Molana, 2023; Pereira, 2018; Song & Valentine, 2024; Stevenson, 2024;

Vitanova, 2024; Warner & Diao, 2022; Zhang & Zhang, 2024). These studies have highlighted a wide range of both implicit and explicit feeling rules while emphasizing the power inequalities embedded in teaching contexts.

3.1.2 Feeling Rules

The concept of feeling rules is closely aligned with the concept of emotion labor and is also indebted to Hochschild's (1979, 1983) groundbreaking work. Feeling rules in a workplace or school are determined by more powerful stakeholders and/or dominant discourses regarding what emotions are "appropriate" to express and to what degree. Benesch and Prior (2023, p. 3) write that Hochschild's "notion of feeling rules as the vehicle that transmits emotion discourses in workplaces … is the clearest manifestation of unequal power." Feeling rules can be explicit, such as the rule for Delta flight attendants in the 1970s to "relax and smile" when contending with difficult and unruly passengers (Hochschild, 1983).

Language teachers more typically contend with implicit feeling rules, such as the need to display professionalism by controlling strong emotional expressions, even when one is frustrated or exhausted (Miller & Gkonou, 2023). While feeling rules can be resisted, teachers often face repercussions for doing so, another indication of how they are folded into the status quo power relations of institutions. As an example, de Oliveira and Barcelos (2024) explore the emotion labor experienced by a teacher of English in Brazil who sought to introduce innovative critical literacy practices in her classroom in a context where teacher reflection and creativity were devalued and efficiency and productivity were rewarded. In this context, the teacher understood that she *should* feel happy about the compliments she received on Brazil's national teacher's day, an "appropriate" emotion associated with this one day of teacher recognition, but instead she felt distressed, indignant, shameful, and even fearful about how national political discourses devalued her efforts and limited she could say or do in her classroom. The conceptual pairing of feeling rules with emotion labor has led researchers to examine how they can move language teachers to maintain or challenge the power relations that shape their institutional, sociocultural, and political worlds.

Benesch (2018, 2020) argued that feeling rules can create significant tensions for individual teachers in their engagement with emotion labor. These tensions may prompt teachers to enact their emotions as a space for agency, allowing them to resist institutional feeling rules by exercising personal agency. In her 2018 study, Benesch examined language teachers' emotion labor in relation to the feeling rules imposed by a university plagiarism policy, focusing on the interplay between emotions and power. Interviews with language teachers about their responses to plagiarism revealed their resistance to these institutional rules and illustrated how emotions became a site for enacting and exercising agency. While complying with the feeling rules required them to engage in emotion labor (e.g. managing frustration or disappointment), teachers' critical engagement with this labor heightened their awareness of both their own emotions and the institutional policies. This awareness, in turn, led to agentive practices, enabling them to resist institutional power and challenge the status quo.

3.1.3 Emotional Capital

Emotional capital conceptualizes emotions as resources that can be accumulated and exchanged for symbolic goods such as supportive relationships, professional confidence, and a strong sense of self-efficacy (Song, 2018). This concept builds on Bourdieu's (1986) notions of cultural and social capital, in which particular forms of cultural knowledge and social relationships are viewed as exchangeable resources that can bring one recognition, prestige, entrance into desirable social networks, and other benefits that support and promote social mobility and bring one a range of advantages. Other scholars have demonstrated how Bourdieu's concepts of symbolic capital and habitus, that is, one's subjective disposition, can apply to teachers' emotions (Zembylas, 2007).

In language education, Song's (2018) study with non-native English-speaking teachers showed how the powerful language ideology of native speakerism positioned these teachers as having diminished authority on linguistic knowledge, which triggered "a deep sense of insecurity" among them (p. 462). She notes that "positive self-image and feelings of professional competence," that is, emotional capital, can be exchanged for "social capital for professional and social networking," while adding that the distribution and circulation of emotional capital in particular social contexts also can "reinforce the status of certain social groups over others" (p. 460). Accumulating emotional capital thus required more emotion labor on their part, compared to their "native-speaker" colleagues, as these teachers sought to gain feelings of confidence in their professional identities. At the same time, those with greater emotional capital often have a greater capacity to undertake emotion labor (Gkonou & Miller, 2021) or exhibit higher engagement in navigating challenging situations such as curriculum reforms (Yang et al., 2022). This line of research demonstrates that the marketplace in which language teacher emotional capital operates creates an unequal field for exchange, indicating that language teachers' accumulating emotional capital for their emotion labor is reduced for some but heightened for others. As a result, the focus of this research shifts from individual teachers' emotional competence, knowledge, or skills to social inequalities in the exchange value of teacher emotions depending on their status and identities.

3.1.4 Vulnerability

Vulnerability is what teachers experience when their "professional identity and moral integrity, as part of being 'a proper teacher,' are questioned and that valued workplace conditions are thereby threatened or lost" (Kelchtermans, 2005, p. 997). In this sense, vulnerability becomes an integral part of teachers' professional lives, playing a significant role in their job satisfaction and performance (Kelchtermans, 2011). Teachers increasingly experience vulnerability when facing school reform mandates and new educational policies, which often require changes in how they teach and perceive their professional identity. Kelchtermans (2011) identified several sources of teacher vulnerability, including policy decisions by educational administrators, relationships within the school (such as interactions with principals, parents, and colleagues), and limitations on teachers' sense of efficacy.

Since vulnerability interacts with structure, identity, and agency (Lasky, 2005), it can have varying effects on teachers. While vulnerability may lead to teacher isolation, burnout, and dropout (Lasky, 2005), some teachers use it as an opportunity to reflect on their teaching conditions and practices, driving changes that improve their professional work environments. In other words, vulnerability can foster self-improvement when teachers have the coping capacity and are able to use it as a means for analyzing and navigating challenging situations. Kelchtermans (2011) identified two key dimensions of vulnerability – the moral and political dimensions – suggesting that understanding and acknowledging these aspects is critical for developing effective coping strategies. The moral dimension of vulnerability relates to a teacher's sense of "being a proper teacher," which involves not only professional skills and competencies but also moral integrity. The political dimension concerns the broader political consequences and the actions taken to maintain or reestablish proper teaching conditions, thereby protecting and reaffirming the teacher's professional identity. This means that teachers' experiences of vulnerability need to be explored within the institutional, social, and discursive contexts where they strive to maintain their professional identity and achieve their teaching goals. These contexts include the policies and administrative decisions that affect their working conditions, the social relationships and power dynamics within their schools, and the broader societal discourse, norms, and biases that define what it means to be a "good teacher." Exploring vulnerability within these intersecting contexts highlights how teachers negotiate tensions between their professional values and external expectations and confront challenges that may arise from conflicting institutional demands. Thus, diverse contexts are reflected in LTE research on vulnerability, including Korean English teachers' vulnerability in relation to the notion of the all-knowing teacher and identity (Song, 2016), challenges surrounding professional identity and visibility on social media (Nejadghanbar et al., 2024), online language teaching (Song, 2022), and transnational teaching contexts (Nazari & Kamali, 2024).

3.1.5 Critical Emotional Reflexivity

Critical emotional reflexivity, as described by Zembylas (2008, 2014), refers to the process of critically examining and reflecting on one's emotional experiences, particularly in relation to power structures, social norms, and ideologies. This concept emphasizes how emotions are socially and politically constructed and how they can either reinforce or challenge power dynamics in various social contexts. In the context of education, critical emotional reflexivity enables teachers and learners to recognize that their emotions are largely influenced and shaped by broader societal forces – such as race, class, gender, and culture – and how these emotions, in turn, influence their identities, relationships, and practices within institutional settings. By critically reflecting on emotions, individuals can become more aware of how their emotional responses might reproduce inequalities, and, as a result, take action to foster more just and equitable practices.

Zembylas (2008, 2014) argues that teachers are not naturally equipped with critical emotional awareness due to the traditional cognitive focus of reflection, which prioritizes effective teaching strategies and skills in teacher education. He suggests that the reflexive process needs to be deliberately guided and supported (see Section 4.2) in order to cultivate a deeper, more critical awareness of the emotional dimensions of educational practice. This approach recognizes the potential for emotions to resist and challenge existing social and educational inequalities for social justice teaching. Ultimately, this notion extends individuals' awareness of their own emotions in relation to power hierarchies, underscoring the intersection of emotions, power, and action. Due to its role in self-development and transformation, the notion has been applied in LTE research to examine how teacher education programs pedagogize emotions in relation to identity and agency – such as in a practicum course in Türkiye (Toker-Bradshaw & Tezgiden-Çakçak, 2024), world language teacher education in the United States (Song, 2025a), and an ESL teacher internship course in the United States (Song & Valentine, 2024).

3.1.6 Feeling Power

Feeling power describes the relationship between power and emotional experiences in two ways: (1) the emotional experience of others' power or authority, and (2) the experience of empowerment. According to Boler (1999), the word "feeling" in the phrase, feeling power, has dual meanings, leading to two distinct roles for emotions. On one hand, feeling as a verb refers to how teachers control their emotions as they feel the power of others and, as a result, become silent. In this sense, feeling power emphasizes the relationship between emotion and power and is closely related to emotion labor. Teachers often adhere to institutional feeling rules by managing or suppressing their emotions to align with expectations of professionalism. Suppressed emotions, such as anxiety and fear, may prevent teachers from addressing challenging situations, potentially shutting down communication and hindering both professional development and personal growth (Lasky, 2005). On the other hand, feeling as a noun refers to one's feelings as a form of power, allowing individuals to use their emotions as a means of resistance against unequal or ineffective social and educational practices. This perspective of feeling power underscores the connection between LTE and agency. For example, Song and Olazabal-Arias (2024) demonstrates how a TL shifted from feeling overpowered by institutional policies in relation to his teacher identity to gaining his own feeling power – emotions as a site of agency – through critically reflecting on and sharing his emotions as part of reflective practice (see Section 4.2).

In Box 2, Juyoung reflects on her experiences researching LTE in relation to some of the concepts discussed in this section.

BOX 2 JUYOUNG'S PERSONAL NARRATIVE ON RESEARCHING LTE

While interest in LTE has grown significantly over the past decade, my own interest in this area was unplanned. I stumbled upon LTE about ten years ago while researching Korean students' early study abroad experiences in English-speaking countries (a phenomenon popularly known as *joki yuhak*). This practice, common among upper middle-class Korean families, involves taking or sending school-age children to English-speaking countries to give them a competitive advantage in developing English proficiency early. At the time, I had been working with several Korean families in the United States and was curious about how these students were performing academically – particularly in English classrooms – after returning to South Korea. I conducted interviews with fourteen secondary English teachers, focusing on the students' performance on English assessments, classroom

Box 2 (cont.)

participation, peer relationships, and the support needed for their readjustment to Korean schools.

What struck me during these interviews was not just the insights about the students, but the emotional responses of the teachers themselves. Many of these teachers, who had extensive teaching experience and had undergone various teacher training programs mandated or supported by the Ministry of Education, began to "outburst" their emotions. They spoke candidly about feelings of shame, regret, anxiety, and disappointment when teaching returnee students in their classrooms. These intense emotional expressions during the interviews led me to a topic I had never considered researching before. I found myself compelled to shift my focus from the returnee students to their teachers, marking the beginning of my exploration into LTE (Song, 2016).

The teachers' emotion-laden interviews raised an important question: Where do their emotions, specifically their anxiety in teaching returnee students, come from? In the Korean educational system, becoming a public-school teacher is highly competitive, involving rigorous processes such as gaining admission to a college of education and passing the highly selective national teacher certification examination. Despite this, the teachers perceived that returnee students possess superior oral fluency and native-like pronunciation, even though they often lack the English skills emphasized in the Korean English curriculum (e.g. prescriptive grammar and lexical knowledge). I realized that the teachers' anxiety about English competence does not stem from measurable English proficiency but rather from societal expectations and collective desires for English fluency among Koreans – commonly referred to as "English fever." This phenomenon is deeply ingrained in Korean society, influencing not only English education but also the broader educational landscape, including other language education (Song & Park, 2019).

Interestingly, I discovered a similar level of anxiety about English competence among Korean language teachers in Korean-only classrooms (Song, 2023). In this context, being native speakers of the Korean language was not sufficient, as the pervasive ideology of English as a global language had extended beyond English classrooms and into other second language classrooms. This realization helped me understand that the teachers' anxiety about English is not merely about a perceived lack of English skills. Instead, it intersects with broader language ideologies,

Box 2 (cont.)

particularly the power and prestige associated with English, which exert significant influence over speakers of other languages in educational contexts.

Since then, I have continued to research LTE, which have become a significant strand of my research agenda. My interest in LTE deepened further through my own experiences of anxiety about English competence, which heightened my sensitivity to social and critical approaches to LTE. Researching LTE not only helped me understand my own emotions but also provided insights into my frequent feelings of anxiety and inferiority stemming from my linguistic background as a non-native speaker of English and my minority status as an Asian faculty member at a US institution. Building on this, I began to explore my emotions more deeply by critically reflecting on the social context of my experiences as a teacher (Song, 2022) and a parent of a bilingual child (Song & Wu, 2024).

Researching my own emotions, as well as those of others, makes me vulnerable and brings forth various personal and ethical challenges. Exploring my own emotions often led to stories I might have preferred to deflect. Sharing and revealing the "personal" aspects of my experiences required heightened self-reflexivity about my actions and the social conditions that shaped my lived experiences of emotions. Re-living those moments and re-experiencing those emotions often came with regret, disappointment, anger, or shame. However, dealing with these emotions during the research process ultimately provided me with new insights and helped me position my identity within the social, cultural, and political context of language teaching. In this sense, researching my emotions enabled me to develop what Zembylas (2008, 2014) calls critical emotional reflexivity. These experiences inspired me to incorporate similar activities in teacher education courses, encouraging TLs to reflect critically on their emotions as part of their professional development, as will be explored in Section 4.

I found researching others' emotions also presented significant ethical questions: How do I have the right to define and describe their emotions? For whom am I conducting research on LTE? These questions led me to focus more on exploring language teachers' lived experiences within social contexts, rather than reducing emotions to simplistic categories such as positive versus negative or similar terms. I also constantly remind myself of the goal of researching LTE. I feel that revealing someone's

> **Box 2 (cont.)**
>
> deeply private experiences can only be justified if it contributes meaningfully to teachers' professional development or to the field by enhancing our understanding of language teachers and their work. These considerations continuously drive me to cultivate researcher reflexivity and to confront the vulnerabilities inherent in my role as a researcher navigating areas fraught with ongoing ethical challenges (see Section 5 for a discussion on researcher reflexivity and research ethics).

3.2 Contributions of the Research

3.2.1 Positioning Emotions in Historical, Cultural, and Ideological Contexts

The most significant contribution of LTE research from critical approaches lies in its examination of individuals' emotions within social structures, tracing their sources to cultural, political, and historical contexts. This approach provides deeper insights into LTE. Moving beyond the question of *"what kinds of emotions"* language teachers experience, this research seeks to address *"why"* they experience those emotions. Specifically, it demonstrates that language teachers' emotions are not isolated individual traits but rather dynamic and discursive constructs. These emotions emerge from and are continuously shaped by intersections with institutional conditions, social structures, ideologies, and power relations. As a result, individuals are understood to experience unequal emotions (Sah, 2023) or uneven emotion labor (Song, 2025b) based on their social, linguistic, and racial backgrounds. This means that certain language teachers may experience more intense feelings of fear, anxiety, shame, and regret as a consequence of their social positioning and status. This aligns closely with discussions of language teacher identity from a discursive perspective (see De Costa & Norton, 2017).

LTE research grounded in critical approaches seeks to trace and examine the sources of "unpleasant" or "negative" emotions within social and power structures. For example, Song (2016) investigated Korean English teachers' experiences of heightened anxiety when teaching students who had studied English abroad. Many teachers in the study perceived these students' English proficiency as superior to their own non-native variety of English, resulting in profound anxiety and shame about their English skills and teaching abilities. These emotions were further intensified by Korean cultural norms that position teachers as all-knowing authorities. Song and Park (2019) further theorized

Korean English teachers' anxiety within the framework of language ideology of English prevalent in Korean society. They examined various government-initiated educational policies that promoted native English speakerism and English immersion education, contributing to the phenomenon of "English fever" among Koreans. Within this context, anxiety about one's English skills becomes "structured" through daily interactions shaped by broader social narratives. In one case, they analyzed the experience of a Korean English teacher with extensive teaching experience who had recently returned from a short professional training program in the United States. While observing teachers in US schools, the participant teacher reported becoming aware of the strong expertise and skills that Korean English teachers possessed and developed compared to teachers elsewhere. These realizations enhanced his professional confidence, enabling him to critically reflect on and resist societal and institutional pressures to achieve native-like English proficiency. The authors pointed out that his newfound confidence was still rooted in his experience of studying abroad in an English-speaking country, specifically the United States. In this sense, his feelings of confidence continued to operate within the dominant ideological framework that positions the United States as the ultimate source of validation for English teachers' skills and abilities. These studies on Korean English teachers highlight how individuals' emotions are socially and ideologically constructed. Emotions do not function as static constraints that bind teachers to a particular ideological position, nor do they allow teachers to be entirely free from the material conditions that underpin those ideologies.

3.2.2 Unraveling the Interplay of Power, Agency, and Emotions

The second major contribution of the research from critical approaches to LTE lies in its capacity to illustrate how language teachers exercise agency within the structural constraints of their pedagogical choices and professional development. In doing so, it frames emotion as a space for ongoing reflection, resistance, and potential change. Research on language teachers' emotion labor and feeling rules specifically examines how teachers enact emotions as a site of agency through critical reflection on their engagement in emotion labor. Rather than presenting a one-dimensional relationship between emotion labor and its potential consequences, such as teacher burnout, isolation, or other "negative" outcomes, this body of research explores the multifaceted nature of emotion labor.

A notable example is research on the multidimensional effects of teacher caring, an emotion relatable to many, if not all, teachers. Teachers' feelings of caring may be genuine and self-initiated, forming an integral part of their personal and professional goals in teaching. While a strong commitment to caring for students can lead to emotional rewards such as satisfaction and/or happiness (Miller & Gkonou, 2018, 2023; Mosqueda, 2025), it can also give rise to a range of emotional struggles, including vulnerability, anxiety, and pain (see also the discussion on emotion-focused pedagogies in Section 4.1). When a certain level of caring is expected or imposed by institutions, teachers' emotion labor is further heightened. For example, Warner and Diao (2022) examined the feeling rules associated with a pedagogy of care that US foreign language teachers implemented during the COVID-19 pandemic. Their analysis of teacher interviews revealed that feeling rules directed teachers to manage and suppress their frustration, disappointment, and other emotions to demonstrate care for their students. This care was expressed through maintaining personal contact with students, fostering a sense of community, regulating student emotions, and supporting their wellbeing beyond the classroom. In adhering to these feeling rules, foreign language teachers engaged in significant emotion labor as they managed their own anxieties, exhaustion, and feelings of isolation. The authors observed that teachers complied with these feeling rules to fulfill their professional responsibility and teacher identity, particularly in the context of declining student enrollment in foreign language programs. This adherence was seen as integral to enhancing student retention and recruitment. Warner and Diao argued that these feeling rules ultimately served institutional goals, as teachers' emotion labor became a means of sustaining foreign language programs amid decreasing enrollments and threats to program viability. Their analysis offers a critical perspective on how language teachers' care for student learning and wellbeing intersects with institutional agendas, creating tensions between institutional feeling rules and teachers' sense of good teaching.

Pereira (2018) also explored the cultural politics of caring as an emotional practice in Singapore's secondary schools under the Ministry of Education's explicit aims for the teaching service – "Lead, Care, Inspire" with "Integrity, Care, and Harmony." In his interviews with secondary English teachers regarding the performance evaluation tool, the Enhanced Performance Management System (EPMS), Pereira found out that the ethic of care played a significant role in teachers' development of subjectivities, beliefs, and practices. Teachers reported that the tensions between the pragmatic and idealized goals of caring teaching were exacerbated by multiple and extensive evaluative criteria used by the EPMS to assess their caring efforts. The author argued that the governmental instrumentality of the ethic of care prioritizes neoliberal imperatives of educational accountability over the stated educational and curricular goals. In this regard, this accountability regime ultimately diminished teacher and student morale, reduced productivity, and even contributed to ill-health among teachers, undermining the very ethos of care it sought to promote.

These two studies effectively demonstrate that feeling rules are not about the emotions themselves (nor simply about emotional management), but rather guide teachers' actions (Hochschild, 1983) – their interactions with students, pedagogical approaches, and professional conduct. This raises an important question about the power of institutional feeling rules over individuals and the role of agency in navigating these constraints. While teachers can enact emotion as a space for agency by resisting those feeling rules through critical reflection during emotion labor (Benesch, 2018), such criticality does not always translate into agentive practice. Agency itself operates within power structures, and teachers' often marginalized and precarious status may place them in a position of compliance, limiting their ability to resist institutional expectations (Her & De Costa, 2022). Alternatively, a form of agency in resisting institutional feeling rules may manifest as the resignation of early career teachers, due to the long-term effects of emotion labor on their elevated burnout and decreased wellbeing (Zhang & Zhang, 2024). Given the complex relationship between agency and emotion, other studies have explored the role of pedagogical practices – such as reflective practices and collaborative dialogue within teacher education programs – in supporting language teachers' enactment of agency through critical emotional reflexivity (see Section 4.2.1).

3.2.3 Highlighting the Emotional Landscape of Teacher Identity

Scholars have argued for greater attention to the emotional dimension of identity within teacher identity research (e.g. De Costa & Norton, 2017), as feeling rules inform teachers' perceptions of what it means to be a "good" teacher and to adopt "appropriate" pedagogies within specific contexts (Zembylas, 2005). The notion of a good teacher extends beyond a cognitive or rationalized understanding; it encompasses teachers' *felt sense* of who they are and how they embody their identity as "good" teachers. Critical approaches to emotions highlight how teacher identity and emotions are mutually dependent and continuously negotiated, constructed, and reconstructed within contexts of dominance, resistance, and social interactions (Zembylas, 2003, 2005).

While the studies discussed in 3.3.2 all touch on teacher identity, several other studies have explicitly documented TLs' emotional experiences during the process of becoming language teachers within teacher education, highlighting the crucial role of the emotional dimension in their identity development (Chen et al., 2022; Gao & Cui, 2022; Ji et al., 2022; Nguyen, 2014; Song, 2021; Teng, 2017; Wolff & De Costa, 2017; Vega & Fallas-Escobar, 2022; Yuan &

Lee, 2014). Song (2021), for example, explored a TL's internship experience in the United States through interviews, observations, and self-reflective statements. The analysis revealed that the TL encountered numerous emotional struggles and tensions, largely due to a dissonance between her theoretical understanding of English language teaching and the realities of classroom practice. Additionally, her observations of perceived unfair practices and negative attitudes toward English learners heightened her emotional challenges. The TLs' efforts to navigate and manage her emotions, both within and beyond the classroom, constituted her emotion labor. Through this process, the TL developed a heightened emotional awareness and resistance to the negative attitudes she observed toward her students, which fostered a deeper emotional reflexivity. This reflexivity enabled her to critically examine and challenge established practices, contributing to the construction and transformation of her teacher identity. The findings suggest that understanding one's emotions in relation to teaching can serve as a catalyst for questioning practices and reshaping teacher identity, offering valuable implications for teacher education. Wolff and De Costa (2017) focused on how a TL's status as a non-native English-speaking teacher (NNEST) led to emotional struggles while enrolled in a US MATESOL program. The participant, Puja, expressed frustration with language policies, ideological biases, institutional norms, and the conflicts these created with her evolving teacher identity. The authors argued that Puja's emotional responses were largely shaped by her status as a NNEST. This status led to a significant decline in her confidence regarding her linguistic competence until she developed strategies to address and manage these tensions. The findings underscored the complex relationship between emotions and teacher identity. Emotions such as anxiety and self-doubt emerged in connection with Puja's perceived NNEST status and the expectations surrounding her proficiency, creating a dissonance between her knowledge acquisition and emotional experiences. These tensions highlighted how emotions influence and interact with the process of teacher identity development.

In the EMI context, Li et al. (2024) conducted a case study exploring the teacher identity of a novice lecturer at a Chinese university. Through the analysis of teacher interviews, self-reflective journals, and digital conversations and posts, the study revealed that emotional discourses played a key role in helping the teacher develop greater awareness of her identity construction. The authors argued that EMI teaching presents dual challenges – both linguistic and pedagogical – as teachers navigate the demands of delivering discipline-specific content while simultaneously enhancing students' English language proficiency. At the outset of the study, the teacher expressed feelings of inadequacy and doubt about her ability to fulfill the role of an EMI teacher. Over time, however, positive feedback and admiration from her students became significant sources of confidence and satisfaction. Her shifting emotional states reflected internal conflicts within her professional identity and guided her toward opportunities for professional development. The study demonstrated that the teacher's sense of failure or success was closely linked to the emotional connections she established with her students. These findings underscore the pivotal role emotions play in shaping a teacher's nuanced understanding of her professional identity, as well as in navigating growth within challenging educational contexts.

Other research explores the complex emotional landscapes of teachers' experiences in relation to various intersectional identity markers such as gender, race, and non-native linguistic status (e.g. Stevenson, 2024; Vitanova, 2024), as well as emerging teaching contexts such as social media (Song & Nejadghanbar, 2024). These studies illustrate that the interplay between emotion and identity in English language teachers is both complex and dynamic, with emotions functioning as both a reflection of and a mediating force behind identity construction. Recognizing and addressing this interrelationship can help language teachers navigate the emotional demands of their profession while fostering a clearer sense of professional identity and personal growth. The research also suggests that understanding the interrelationship between emotion and identity can meaningfully inform teacher education and professional development.

3.3 Implications and Suggestions

Interviews and reflective journals served as the primary data sources in critical approaches. These methods enable researchers to uncover emotions that are often invisible or hidden from outsiders by guiding participants to reflect on and report emotional experiences tied to specific events and situations, thereby capturing their lived emotional experiences in relation to teaching contexts, power dynamics, and inequalities. To deepen participants' reflections, the questions and prompts used in interviews and reflective narratives went beyond simply asking what emotions were experienced. They also included *why* questions to uncover participants' perceptions and reasoning concerning their emotional experiences.

Interviews, in particular, are described as "meaning-making encounters" (Gkonou & Miller, 2021, p. 141) between interviewees and interviewers. In these encounters, meanings are not simply conveyed by the interviewees but are collaboratively constructed through their interaction. Interviewers are seen as active participants (Holstein & Gubrium, 2003), engaging in reflection, remembering, and reconstructing experiences and meanings. In this process, they may mediate and reinterpret the knowledge and realities they have encountered. At the same time, the interview questions provide interviewees with opportunities to reflect on their emotional experiences – reflections that might not have occurred without the specific prompts provided by the researchers (Gkonou & Miller, 2021). This demands heightened researcher reflexivity on the part of the interviewer. Interviewers must actively engage in the interview process, skillfully shifting between their roles as teachers and researchers to make sense of interviewees' experiences. This involves deep reflexivity, where researchers critically reflect on both their own emotional experiences and those of the respondents.

As this section has demonstrated, LTE is never independent of social structures (Ahmed, 2004; Boler, 1999). Therefore, it is essential to remember that emotions are inherently neither positive nor negative (Zembylas, 2003). For example, research concepts such as vulnerability and emotion labor are not always negative. Rather, they are multidimensional and dynamic experiences that can lead to either teacher agency and transformation or teacher isolation and burnout (Lasky, 2005; Zembylas, 2003).

At the same time, wellbeing is not simply the opposite of vulnerability or emotion labor. Wellbeing is also a complex emotional experience, influenced by both individual factors and social and contextual elements (Mercer, 2021). Teachers' experiences of wellbeing vary depending on their personal and professional histories, goals, perceived social positions, competence, and the level of organizational support they receive. For example, many teachers who willingly engage in emotion labor to show care for their students often experiencing emotional rewards that enhance their wellbeing (Gkonou & Miller, 2021; Miller & Gkonou, 2018, 2023; Mosqueda, 2025).

To deepen the understanding of the affective dimensions of language teaching, teacher identity, and professional trajectories, it is essential to have a clear and accurate application of relevant concepts when researching LTE from a critical perspective. For example, Benesch and Prior (2023) caution against equating emotional stress and struggles with emotion labor. They emphasize the critical and feminist roots of the concept and call for greater awareness of language teaching contexts as workplaces that are hierarchically organized. The management of emotions, according to feeling rules, not only reflects power inequalities but also serves the interests of specific groups (e.g. institutions and employers) (Benesch & Prior, 2023; Hochschild, 1983). Benesch and Prior (2023) also noted a power imbalance between researchers and language teachers in teacher emotion research, warning researchers against categorizing teachers' emotions as either positive or negative. They stated, "When emotions are sorted into positive and negative categories and hypothesized as good and bad respectively in research contexts, feeling rules are imposed from the exalted status of researchers studying practitioners, a long-established hierarchy in applied linguistics and other fields" (p. 7).

With these considerations in mind, more empirical research should focus on context-specific and nuanced interpretations of teachers' emotional experiences. Future studies could explore how power dynamics, including the ideology of emotion, operate across institutional and cultural contexts, or among individuals within a given context, taking into account factors such as gender, age, and social and linguistic backgrounds. Additionally, research could examine how culture-specific feeling rules direct teachers' emotional experiences and their management of emotions throughout their personal and professional development.

4 Pedagogical Approaches

As seen in previous sections, LTE research – regardless of its approach – has emphasized the crucial role emotions play in negotiating and developing teacher identity and practice. It highlights the importance of supporting teachers' emotional wellbeing and providing related professional development opportunities. However, a notable gap remains in understanding how emotions are systematically integrated into teacher education practices. To date, limited research has explored pedagogical approaches to emotions, leaving an open question about how teacher educators can meaningfully incorporate emotional engagement into their instructional practices (Nazari et al., 2024; Nazari & Hu, 2024; Song, 2025a; Song & Olazabal-Arias, 2024; Song & Valentine, 2024; Yazan, 2023, 2025). This gap suggests that addressing emotions in teacher education remains relatively rare (Zembylas, 2005; though see Eraldemir-Tuyan, 2019; Golombek & Doran, 2014).

In this section, we discuss pedagogical approaches that incorporate critical reflection on emotions and offer suggested activities. We begin by introducing four relevant pedagogies that explicitly focus on and utilize emotions in teaching, enabling TLs and teacher educators to explore the complex entanglement between emotions and social contexts. The following sections provide pedagogical activities and sample reflective questions applicable to teacher education contexts. Finally, the narrative box in this section features a dialogue between us on emotions, pedagogy, and language teacher education.

4.1 Relevant Pedagogies

The following pedagogical approaches presented emphasize TLs' critical engagement with emotions, offering critical perspectives that largely align with Freire's (2017) concept of critical pedagogy. Freire's critical pedagogy aims to empower students to critically examine power structures and social inequalities within social and educational contexts. Central to this approach is active dialogue, which fosters students' awareness of their own social realities – a process known as *conscientização* – and motivates them to work toward social transformation. Critical pedagogy rejects the traditional "banking model" of education, where teachers simply deposit information into students. Instead, it advocates for a "problem-posing" approach, in which students and teachers co-construct knowledge through critical reflection and action. In this approach, dialogue becomes a mutual learning process, encouraging both students and teachers to interrogate assumptions and engage in transformative learning.

From this perspective, pedagogy transcends a narrow view of instruction focused solely on teaching methods. Instead, it embraces a broader, socially engaged, and transformative approach, positioning education as a means of fostering critical consciousness and social change.

4.1.1 Pedagogy of Love

The pedagogy of love suggests that teaching involves not only transmitting information and skills but also fostering love, addressing learners as whole individuals (Freire, 2017; hooks, 1994). This view integrates love as part of a holistic pedagogical approach, evolving in response to the needs of individuals and specific contexts (Freire, 2017; hooks, 1994; Zembylas, 2017). In line with this perspective, *pedagogical love,* as discussed by Lanas and Zembylas (2015), involves genuine care, trust, and empathy for a student's learning and growth. It is seen as an emotion that entails vulnerability and risk in teaching as it requires making pedagogical choices rooted in individual teaching philosophies and ethics, formed by situational and broader contextual factors. From this viewpoint, pedagogical love is a relational and political practice informed by social, historical, and cultural contexts, ultimately aiming for praxis, as "love is what love does" (Lanas, 2017, p. 565). For example, pedagogical love can involve teachers demonstrating care, empathy, and understanding toward refugee students, extending beyond subject-area instruction. It can be cultivated through teacher–student interactions in various ways, even when there is limited shared language (Kaukko *et al.*, 2021; Zaidi *et al.*, 2021). Pedagogical practices that nurture a supportive classroom environment and foster a sense of belonging become increasingly vital, particularly in diverse and challenging educational contexts

In the field of language education, some studies have extended the conceptual discussion of "love" or "pedagogical love" (e.g. Barcelos & Coelho, 2016;

Wang et al., 2022), while others have explored language teachers' lived experiences with pedagogical love. For example, Li and Rawal (2018) examined the experiences of an EMI teacher in China and an English teacher in Nepal, highlighting how their love for the profession sustained their investment in teaching. However, this love was deeply shaped by local and broader teaching conditions, which in turn either fostered growth or contributed to burnout over time. Barcelos (2020) also analyzed the narrative of a Brazilian student teacher in her search for *revolutionary love* – a critical form of love that functions as a transformative force (Chabot, 2008). The study revealed that the student teacher's sense of love was tied to the pursuit of peace and was instrumental in shaping her professional identity development.

In her recent review of pedagogical love in ELT, Barcelos (2025) observed that numerous studies in language education tend to treat pedagogical love as a measurable variable compared to those in general education, often framing it as an extension of positive psychology. For example, Derakhshan et al. (2023) investigated 773 EFL teachers from various countries using three psychometric instruments: the Disposition Toward Loving Pedagogy (DTLP), the Teaching for Creativity Scale (TCS), and the Utrecht Work Engagement Scale (UWES). Similarly, Zhi and Wang (2023) explored possible interrelationships among EFL teachers' creativity, professional success, and loving pedagogy in a study involving 322 Chinese EFL teachers. This perspective aligns pedagogical love with broader concepts such as positive emotions, learner wellbeing, and peace, reflecting the growing influence of positive psychology in language learning research. However, Barcelos (2025) argues that pedagogical love is more than a set of variables; rather, it is an approach – "a self-regulated, goal-oriented commitment" (p. 271) that involves passion, sacrifice, pain, and empathy. She cautions against viewing pedagogical love as a universal practice that should be implemented by all teachers. Because it often entails emotion labor and vulnerability, mandating pedagogical love risks reinforcing feeling rules, which may undermine teachers' autonomy and emotional authenticity.

4.1.2 Pedagogy of Hope

The pedagogy of hope (Freire, 2021; hooks, 1994) nurtures hope and optimism to make pedagogy transformative and action-oriented. Freire's notion of hope is not about wishful thinking or naive disregard for reality, but begins with critical attitudes, or *conscientização* (critical consciousness), which involves recognizing what is lacking in one's current situation and acknowledging the reality of oppression. This form of critical hope drives action toward transforming the status quo for a more just and equitable future. Both Freire and hooks argued that dreaming of change is imperative, and these dreams, grounded in hope, require critical reflection and awareness.

In language education, Imperiale et al. (2017) incorporated Freire's critical notion of hope into a teacher education course in Gaza, Palestine. The online course aimed to support participants' professional development in language teaching while encouraging the creation of localized teaching practices through the use of Palestinian arts. Through collaboration with the researchers, participants reflected on and co-constructed critical and creative language pedagogies. They developed teaching materials grounded in local cultural contexts, including Palestinian-themed cartoons, poems in both English and Palestinian Arabic, traditional songs translated into English, as well as videos, clips, and role-plays. The authors reported that this practice enabled participants to embrace language education as a means of nurturing critical hope and fostering peaceful resistance, while rejecting the view of language as a rigid system of standardized skills. They argued that the pedagogy of critical hope implemented in the project emphasized the transformative power of educational praxis, demonstrating how language education can serve as a space for identity affirmation, cultural expression, and sociopolitical engagement.

In a more recent study, Sembiante and Tian (2023) explored how translanguaging serves as a pedagogy of hope, supporting learning, fostering participation, and deepening connections with linguistically diverse practices. Their concept of a "pedagogy of translanguaging hope" frames translanguaging as a hopeful approach that challenges monoglossic perspectives and practices among teachers and students. They argue that translanguaging embodies *heteroglossic hope* through multilingual and multimodal approaches, countering monoglossic bias by enhancing students' cognition and language learning while creating inclusive entry points for all members of learning communities. As a result, Sembiante and Tian contend that translanguaging facilitates more just, equitable, and humanizing instructional practices in multilingual classrooms. Similarly, Zayas-Santiago and Smith (2024) explored how Latinx teachers' translanguaging practices, informed by their multilingual and multicultural experiences, served as transformative resources of hope for minority students in US schools. The authors argued that these teachers, by positioning themselves in contrast to "that teacher" – a representation of a normative monolingual educator who disregards or suppresses multilingualism – were able to affirm and leverage their students' linguacultural identities. Through this stance, they cultivated a pedagogy rooted in hope and resistance, instilling and transforming their students' stance and identity toward hope.

4.1.3 Pedagogy of Discomfort

The pedagogy of discomfort encourages learners to engage with the discomfort and tensions arising from difficult discussions, particularly those related to conflict in classrooms and beyond. Boler (1999) describes it as a purposeful examination of uncomfortable emotions that individuals might otherwise "resist or deflect, such as defensive anger, fear of change, the fear of losing personal or cultural identity, as well as guilt and discomfort that arise when our beliefs and assumptions are challenged" (p. 176). These challenging discussions push learners to confront the tension between their personal beliefs, attitudes, and normalized practices on one hand, and the realities of social structures and institutional power on the other (Zembylas, 2012). This pedagogy considers the emotion of discomfort as a function operating between individuals and their sociopolitical surroundings, particularly in relation to issues of power and inequality (Boler, 1999; Boler & Zembylas, 2003).

By embracing discomfort, TLs are better positioned to challenge the institutional constraints on their understanding of themselves, both individually and collectively. Similarly, TLs are encouraged to step out of their comfort zones and engage with discomfort as a means of critically examining inherited beliefs and assumptions. This approach has been applied in teacher education to explore the pedagogical potential of discomfort in addressing issues such as ethnic and religious conflict, racism, colonialism, migration, and social exclusion (e.g. Cutri & Whiting, 2015; Ohito, 2016; Zembylas & McGlynn, 2012; Zembylas & Papamichael, 2017).

In language education, the pedagogy of discomfort seeks to expose the subtle ways in which commonly accepted teaching practices marginalize diverse cultural and linguistic knowledge (Cabiles, 2021) or overlook critical social and cultural perspectives in world language classrooms (Porto & Zembylas, 2024). Recent research also explores the use of literature and the arts as tools for addressing social and political issues. For example, Porto and Zembylas (2024) employed literature and the arts to engage with traumatic and painful representations in language classrooms, transforming the classroom into a space where teachers and students confront stories of loss, injury, pain, and trauma. Similarly, Sun's (2023) study in China demonstrated how explicit teacher guidance enabled English learners to critically engage with difficult sociopolitical issues – such as global human rights violations and empathy – through literature and the arts in language learning. By fostering critical reflection on such practices, the pedagogy of discomfort invites language educators and learners to confront their unease, interrogate dominant ideologies, and reimagine more inclusive and socially just approaches to language education through critical engagement and creativity.

4.1.4 Pedagogy of Empathy

The pedagogy of empathy is another critical pedagogical approach that explores the role of emotions, specifically empathy, in education. *False empathy* (Delgado, 1996) occurs when empathy is shared with good intentions but primarily for the sake of achieving positive outcomes or mutual interests. This type of empathy, though well-meaning, can lead to conflicts and contradictions in TLs' emotional experiences. The concept of false empathy was initially introduced to describe the intentions of White teachers striving to be effective educators of racially, culturally, and linguistically diverse students in decolonial and anti-racist teaching contexts. Despite their good intentions, these teachers often face tensions between their perceptions of empathy's relevance in teaching and the practical challenges of implementing it (Warren, 2015).

To avoid false empathy, teachers and teacher educators must adopt a critical perspective to their emotional experiences. This approach, sometimes referred to as *strategic empathy*, emphasizes the importance of using empathy in both critical and intentional ways (Zembylas, 2012). Strategic empathy involves understanding and expressing empathy while being aware of the power dynamics, biases, and institutional structures that shape emotional experiences in educational settings.

The pedagogy of empathy underscores that emotions, including empathy, should be critically examined within their specific institutional contexts, which influence how emotional support is provided and received. In other words, emotions cannot be simply categorized as positive or negative; rather, they must be understood through a critical lens that considers their social, cultural, and institutional contexts. This perspective challenges teachers and teacher educators to engage with emotions not only as personal experiences but also as deeply situated within broader educational and social systems.

In Box 3, we discuss our views on incorporating LTE into language teacher education programs.

BOX 3 DIALOGUE ON PEDAGOGIES FOR LTE IN LANGUAGE TEACHER EDUCATION

Juyoung: While significant advances have been made in researching and understanding LTE, the role of emotions in language teacher education remains underexplored. This gap may stem from the long-standing tradition in language teacher education, which emphasizes rational decision-making, skill development, and a strong teacher knowledge base. However, as research findings in this area continue to grow, they increasingly urge language teacher education to address affect and emotions as integral components of teacher education practices. Given this background, how do you feel about incorporating emotions into language teacher education? Do you think it is necessary?

Box 3 (cont.)

Liz: I do think it is necessary! As we were working on this Element, I found that over and over again researchers were urging language teacher educators to incorporate material on emotions into their training materials and activities. I suspect one reason many teacher educators haven't done so is just lack of time or space. Their programs are already jam-packed, and they can only cover so much material. It also isn't as simple as just adding a lecture or unit to an existing program. Learning about and reflecting on emotions with TLs often requires one-on-one or small group interactions. Teacher educators need to spend time responding carefully and sensitively to TLs' reflections. And to be effective, this kind of reflection and response work needs time. I've been impressed by the longitudinal studies I've read, such as those drawing on Vygotsky's notion of *perezhivanie*. This work shows how effective teacher educators can be in mediating TLs' understanding of emotions and their professional growth, but it definitely needs to be sustained over time to be effective. It's also important to recognize that this kind of work asks a lot of everyone involved. It requires a degree of emotional vulnerability from the teacher educators themselves, and that can feel risky.

Juyoung: Definitely! Although scholars generally agree on the importance of addressing emotions in language teacher education, there is less consensus on which emotions should be prioritized and how they should be addressed. I believe that this is an area that warrants further research in the future. Do you think teacher educators should focus on particular emotions?

Liz: I think that focusing on how to create positive and supportive learning environments for TLs' (future) students can be beneficial. The research based in positive psychology can be useful for helping TLs recognize their emotional strengths and for learning about strategies that can help them deal with emotional challenges. However, I think that it is more important to meet TLs where they are. I remember feeling so unsure about whether I was doing it "right" when I first started teaching. If TLs learn that their feelings of vulnerability, frustration, and uncertainty are not only normal but can actually be treated as resources for learning and growth, I think that they will feel reassured and also more motivated to continue pursuing a career in language teaching. It seems to me that if we treat emotions as worthy of reflection and intellectual engagement, then the squeamishness some TLs might feel about "admitting" to their

Box 3 (cont.)

vulnerabilities can be lessened. I'm pretty sure that I would have benefited enormously from learning about how to practice critical reflection on my emotional experiences when I was a novice teacher. TLs who do learn how to critically reflect on their emotional experiences will be so much better prepared for their professional work. The question is how should emotions be addressed in teacher education. Do you have any insights on this?

Juyoung: I think it varies among teacher educators and teacher education programs. Some scholars and teacher educators emphasize fostering a more positive and supportive learning environment by focusing on strengths, positive emotions, and building resilience, rather than addressing the emotional struggles and challenges that teachers might face. Others advocate for instilling critical perspectives on emotions, teaching conditions, and broader social issues by bringing suppressed and hidden feelings to the forefront for examination. I have been working on several projects with language teachers aimed at their professional development through critical inquiry into their emotions by employing the pedagogy of discomfort for their development of critical emotional reflexivity. When I submitted a research report on the process and outcomes of this pedagogy, one reviewer raised ethical concerns about the approach. The reviewer questioned, "*Is it ethical for teacher educators to awaken teachers' awareness of their suppressed emotions related to unfair conditions?*" They also asked, "*Will this help them find solutions, or will it leave them more dissatisfied with their jobs?*" These questions "haunted" me and prompted deeper reflection. I believe the answers depend on individual beliefs and perspectives. For me, when it comes to ethics, ignoring TLs' emotional struggles is no more ethical than addressing them – particularly when there is a clear pedagogical goal, praxis, and potential for transformation. I consider this commitment to addressing emotions an essential aspect of my own positionality both as a teacher and a researcher as my ultimate goal in teaching is to empower language learners and teachers.

Liz: I completely agree! The work that you have done in working with TLs is so admirable. At the same time, I think it is important for teacher educators to acknowledge and perhaps be reassured that critical reflexivity inevitably involves learning from their own shortcomings. They won't always get it right when working with TLs. Being vulnerable with TLs in terms of their own emotional challenges, through collaborative dialogue, creates a space for genuine connection and learning to emerge. Given this inherent vulnerability for teacher educators as they work with TLs,

> Box 3 (cont.)
>
> perhaps through autoethnographic narratives or by engaging in critical dialogue with them, what do you think teacher educators need to consider when incorporating emotion into their teacher education practices?
>
> **Juyoung**: I think that discussing emotions is not an easy task and must be approached with care and sensitivity. When discussing difficult topics with TLs, I often face ethical dilemmas in balancing the discomfort such discussions might cause them against the potential pedagogical benefits. I understand that addressing challenging emotions could surface feelings TLs prefer to avoid, potentially further marginalizing their identities and professional work. However, I also believe that avoiding these uncomfortable conversations could result in emotion labor, as they suppress their emotions, ultimately leading to teacher burnout and dropout (Zembylas, 2005). There is always a risk in pedagogizing emotions in language teacher education, and it is important to recognize this risk. To me, I am willing to take this risk because I believe that fully committing to my own vulnerability is a crucial aspect of my pedagogical approach to emotions. My commitment stems from my teaching goal of empowering language teachers and learners, along with my ongoing reflexivity on confronting both my personal and professional vulnerabilities – vulnerabilities that emerge from facing who I am and what I strive to do (Brantmeier, 2013). However, I also recognize that each teacher educator brings their own pedagogical goals grounded in their teacher training, identity, and teaching philosophy. While my approach centers on vulnerability, empowerment, and reflexivity, other educators may prioritize different aspects of teacher education practice. Not everyone needs to focus on emotions or adopt similar pedagogical approaches. Yet, when teacher educators do incorporate emotions into their teaching practices, they should commit to their approaches, ensuring their choices are intentional and grounded in their pedagogical values and goals. By doing so, they can foster TLs' meaningful learning experiences, leading to professional development.

4.2 Pedagogical Activities and Reflective Questions

The pedagogies explored in Section 4.1 emphasize praxis through critical reflection on one's emotions in relation to teaching conditions and social structures. They position emotion as a space for critical inquiry, fostering actions aimed at individual and social transformation. The concepts of love, hope, discomfort, and empathy in these pedagogies are not static, simplistic categories that can be neatly labeled as positive or negative. For example, the pedagogy of hope interrogates feelings such as discomfort, fear, despair, or anger in relation to current circumstances before cultivating hope for a better future. Similarly, the pedagogy of love engages with feelings of vulnerability and risk, striving to transmit love and fulfill its transformative purpose. Even empathy, often considered a positive emotion, can take on a negative dimension when expressed as false empathy. These pedagogies call for a critical examination of emotions through contextual and discursive lenses, moving beyond binary categorizations of positive and negative emotions.

Researchers in language education have documented pedagogical activities that support TLs' critical reflection on emotions through critical autoethnographic narratives (Song & Olazabal-Arias, 2024; Yazan, 2023, 2025), collaborative dialogue (Song & Valentine, 2024), and reflective journals (Nazari et al., 2024; Nazari & Hu, 2024).

In the following section, we discuss two teacher education practices that can foster critical reflection and provide example reflective questions. Finally, we offer additional pedagogical considerations for language teacher educators as they strive to implement relevant pedagogies and practices.

4.2.1 Critical Autoethnographic Narratives

Critical autoethnography is a qualitative research method that uses personal narratives to analyze cultural practices (Adams et al., 2015; Chang, 2008). It provides a way to examine the complexities of culture and communication through the lens of the researcher's own experiences. Building on this research method, critical autoethnographic narrative (CAN) is a pedagogical tool utilized by Yazan (2019, 2023, 2024) to promote identity-oriented TESOL teacher preparation. CAN is based on critical language teacher education (Hawkins & Norton, 2009), autoethnography as an account of identity development (Canagarajah, 2012), narrative as a teacher learning tool (Johnson & Golombek, 2011) and identity construction (Barkhuizen, 2016). Compared to autobiographies in the form of journal entries, one of the most frequently used methods in teacher education, CAN is carried out as an ongoing narrative by a TL throughout their coursework and internship and focuses on deconstructing the dominant discourses affecting their identity and pedagogy (Yazan, 2024). It not only documents personal experiences, but examines them from a critical perspective in the process of becoming language teachers and the entanglements of their identity and emotions in such development.

Yazan (2023), for example, documented and analyzed a TL's (Rachel's) CAN in a linguistics course to explore how the guided and iterative process of writing CAN supported Rachel's teacher identity development. The findings revealed how Rachel's emotional experiences, grounded in her storied narratives, contributed to her understanding of her language teacher identity. Additionally, CAN facilitated Rachel's ability to discuss and reflect on her emotions and identity in relation to meso- and macro-level ideologies within her language learning and teaching experiences. Yazan thus contends that CAN is a valuable tool for both researching TLs' identity development and serving as a pedagogy to support TLs' understanding of their emotions in learning and using languages, navigating the university's institutional landscape, and teaching and learning to teach English.

4.2.2 Collaborative Dialogue

Collaborative dialogue between a TL and a teacher educator/mentor, or between peers, provides an avenue for TLs to reflect on and share their felt emotions. It can also be combined with reflective journals or narratives to prevent teacher reflections from becoming repetitive or cyclical. To create a space for collaborative dialogue that is both "safe" for uncovering and sharing emotions and "critical" for fostering praxis, Zembylas (2012) recommends that teachers employ pedagogies of strategic empathy and solidarity alongside the pedagogy of discomfort (Boler, 1999).

Feelings of empathy between a TL and a teacher educator emphasize fostering emotional solidarity, which can support teachers' understanding of their own and others' emotions and builds emotional awareness. Emotional solidarity also helps TLs feel safe enough to share and discuss their emotional experiences. To avoid falling into false empathy, teacher educators must engage in critical inquiry into their own emotions and, when necessary, share their emotional experiences and perspectives on the intersection of power and emotion in institutional contexts (cf. Golombek, 2015).

Collaborative dialogue should also cultivate TLs' ability to embrace and address discomfort and tensions that arise when confronting the "ugly feelings" encountered in classrooms and schools. These difficult discussions challenge teachers to confront conflicts between their personal beliefs, attitudes, and normalized practices on one hand, and broader social structures and institutional power on the other (Zembylas, 2012).

For example, in Song and Valentine (2024), a TL engaged in reflective journaling about emotionally significant events, followed by collaborative dialogue with her mentor. This process helped her develop a critical perspective on the social context of her emotion labor. Through this dialogue, she became empowered to take a more active role when working with content teachers, advocating for her students' needs and improving emotionally draining work conditions. The dialogue required her to take action to address and change challenging work situations. Despite emotional discomfort and other contextual challenges, her commitment to "moving forward" (p. 18) underscored her dedication to both her students' needs and her professional growth. This process also facilitated the development of critical emotional reflexivity, as the teacher was able to articulate and understand the sources of her emotion labor with careful attention to her lived experiences. Through this process, she moved beyond her comfort zone, embracing emotional discomfort as a catalyst for personal and professional transformation.

4.2.3 Reflective Narratives

For the emotions experienced by TLs to serve as catalysts for critical reflection and professional development – rather than being viewed as barriers (Talbot & Mercer, 2018) – we suggest that TLs critically reflect on their emotions by questioning their origins, contexts, and implications. They should also learn to evaluate and share their insights.

To support TLs' critical reflection, reflective questions should focus on a specific aspect of their lives and work. Examples include teacher collaboration (Song & Valentine, 2024), language policy (Her & De Costa, 2022), or extracurricular responsibilities (Song, 2025a). This focused exploration facilitates a deeper examination of emotional experiences and their relevance to social contexts. Box 4 shows some example reflection questions.

Box 4 Reflection questions

- How did you feel during a specific time or situation in school or your classroom?
- How did you feel about a particular activity or your engagement in it?
- How might these feelings be related to your background, relationships with students and colleagues, or school policies? (Would your experiences differ if you had a different racial, gender, linguistic, or social background?)
- How might these feelings connect to broader societal issues beyond the school setting? (Would your experiences differ in a different school or teaching context?)
- Did these feelings influence your teaching? If so, how?

> Box 4 (cont.)
> - Did these feelings influence your relationships with students, peers, or colleagues? If so, how?
> - Did these feelings influence how you see yourself as a teacher? How did they influence your professional development and goals?
> - Do you think your feelings might change over time?
> - Do you plan to address the situations linked to your feelings? If so, how?
> - How do you anticipate changes in your practices or situations will influence your feelings?
>
> Adapted from Song (2025c)

It is important to acknowledge that individuals vary in their willingness and capacity for emotional reflection, which are influenced by personal histories and orientations (Isenbarger & Zembylas, 2006). This variability underscores the notion that "no pedagogy of discomfort can be known a priori" (Zembylas & McGlynn, 2012, p. 45), meaning that no single pedagogy will fit all learners or contexts. Rather, reflective practice must remain flexible, responsive, and context-sensitive, adapting to the diverse emotional experiences and backgrounds of TLs. Setting universal goals for outcomes may be neither feasible nor desirable. Instead, the focus should be on encouraging individual TLs to reflect on their unique backgrounds and experiences, fostering their ability to recognize their emotions and the inequalities surrounding them.

By engaging in this process, TLs can develop a deeper understanding of the social and emotional dimensions of their teaching experiences. Ultimately, this reflection empowers them to articulate their own professional development goals, aligning their reflective practices with their evolving identities and commitments as educators.

4.3 Other Considerations

Critical pedagogies of emotions, as discussed in this section, require heightened commitment and responsibility from teacher educators. The outcomes of TL's critical reflection on their emotions also depend on reciprocal commitment and empathetic connections with teacher educators (Zembylas & McGlynn, 2012). These pedagogies are inherently risky, as they demand significant emotional investment and can take a toll on both teacher educators and TLs. Therefore, pedagogical choices should closely align with teacher educators' identities and their teaching goals (Kanno & Stuart, 2011; Morgan, 2004). Teacher educators' experiences of vulnerability, emotional ambivalence, and emotion labor – particularly when navigating discomforting discourses and offering empathy and hope – reflect their willingness and commitment to achieving the goals of their teaching.

Teacher educators must also recognize that successful teacher education and mentoring inherently involve emotionality, as emotions provide tangible evidence of identity processing (Hargreaves, 2001; Zembylas, 2003). For instance, attempting to support TLs' professional development while avoiding emotional engagement and focusing solely on skills and knowledge in language teacher education can exacerbate struggles and conflicts arising from the gap between classroom realities and educational theories. Avoiding personalized engagement with TLs is unlikely to result in meaningful mentoring, as effective mentoring fundamentally depends on building supportive relationships between teacher educators and TLs. Authentic, learner-centered teacher education practices that prioritize TLs' wellbeing and needs often evoke strong emotions in teacher educators. Therefore, teacher educators must recognize the emotional demands of their role and acknowledge their emotional involvement with TLs as an integral part of the mentoring process.

It is essential for teacher educators to maintain a keen awareness of their identities as language teacher educators and engage in critical reflexivity about their emotions to implement these pedagogies successfully. Despite the centrality of teacher educators' emotions in the pedagogical process, research on the emotions of language teacher educators remains scarce (see De Costa & Nazari, forthcoming). To better understand how the pedagogies described in this section could benefit TLs, more studies are needed that focus on the interplay of emotional experiences between language teacher educators and TLs throughout the pedagogical process. Such research should explore how emotions are co-constructed, negotiated, and reciprocally influence both parties, and how they contribute to TLs' identity development and professional growth.

5 Ethical Considerations and Future Directions

In this Element, we explored LTE from various perspectives and examined its pedagogical potential in supporting language teachers' personal and professional development, as well as their wellbeing. Our discussion of LTE research specifically reflects the current state of the field, which is becoming increasingly diverse in terms of methods, research participants and locations, and ways of conceptualizing emotions. Additionally, LTE research aligns with a broader trend: a shift from focusing on external, explicit factors to examining the more implicit and dynamic aspects of language education. This shift involves moving beyond a focus on language teaching as merely the skills and strategies teachers employ to exploring who language teachers are – particularly in terms of their identity, beliefs, agency, and emotions – and how these aspects intersect with their work. This shift is especially valuable in deepening our understanding of the work of language teachers, offering nuanced insights into the emotional landscape of language teaching.

Our final section of this *Element* centers on our reflections on researcher reflexivity, ethical considerations in LTE research, and our suggestions for future directions to deepen and broaden LTE research.

5.1 Researcher Reflexivity

As teaching is inherently an emotional practice (Hargreaves, 1998), whether through the expression or management of emotions, our discussion on the intersection of research and practice underscores the importance of fostering (critical) emotional reflexivity among both language educators and researchers in language education. As seen in Section 4, we explored the significance of emotional reflexivity in helping TLs understand their emotions in relation to teaching conditions and broader social structures.

Equally important is researchers' reflexivity – their ability to critically examine how their own assumptions, experiences, and positionality influence the research process and its outcomes. Reflexivity involves turning back to oneself and critically examining one's role in the process of building and producing knowledge, making this process itself a central focus of investigation (May & Perry, 2014). In other words, our role in researching LTE, or undertaking any other social inquiry, is not about collecting and uncovering social facts or emotional realities based solely on expertise and scientific analysis. Rather, LTE research is inherently interpretive, meaning that researchers' perspectives – especially given the diverse approaches to emotions – play a significant role in their analyses and findings.

Therefore, it is crucial for researchers to acknowledge their own role in mediating and interpreting research outcomes through a reflexive, analytic lens. This reflexivity informs the direction of the research and even researchers' own understanding of emotions. By engaging in this process, researchers can ensure that their study aligns with their positionality, thus avoiding potential issues arising from misalignment between research topics and epistemology. For example, a researcher who adopts an individual psychological approach to emotions – as measurable, empirical realities – may face challenges when investigating social concepts such as feeling rules and emotion labor using purely quantitative methods like surveys with numerical scales. Since these topics are deeply subjective, context-dependent, and socially constructed, such an approach may lead to oversimplified findings that fail to capture the complexity of teachers' emotional experiences.

Another essential aspect of reflexivity is the interrelationship between social inquiry and its effects on social life (Beck et al., 1994; Giddens, 1984), particularly the dynamic interactions between researchers and participants. As Giddens (1984) conceptualizes in the "double hermeneutic" (p. 374), social inquiry does not merely observe reality but also actively influences the perspectives and behaviors of both the researched and the researchers themselves. This is particularly relevant in LTE research, where scholars engage with participants' emotion-laden experiences, potentially leading to deeper reflections on their own emotions and experiences. Such engagement may result in new understandings and shifts in perspectives, often in ways that are unintentional but which can be meaningfully profound. Therefore, researchers of LTE should anticipate and be open to unexpected changes that may arise during their engagement in LTE research.

Similarly, the research process also affects participating teachers, impacting how they view and experience their emotions and social contexts. This potentially transformative aspect of research underscores the importance of ethical responsibility, requiring researchers to exercise careful and critical attention to the unintended consequences of their work. Thus, LTE researchers must cultivate a heightened awareness of how their inquiry not only generates knowledge but also engages with and alters the lived realities of those involved – whether participants or researchers themselves.

5.2 Research Ethics Concerning LTE

Researching others' deeper and often hidden aspects of their lives – especially as constructed by experiences within institutional relationships – requires more than self-awareness or critical reflection on the part of the researcher. It demands an ethical commitment to addressing the potential impact of the research findings on participants and their broader social contexts. Without such considerations, reflexivity risks becoming a purely intellectual exercise rather than a tool for fostering ethical responsibility in research practices.

Researching someone else's emotions requires more than simply glossing over data to achieve descriptive and analytical neatness that aligns with researchers' agendas. While the foundational principles of research ethics (which are not the scope of this Element; see Hammersley & Traianou, 2012) remain relevant in LTE research, a unique challenge lies in the processes and outcomes of accessing and revealing what is deeply personal and internal.

One significant ethical challenge in LTE research is the risk of oversimplifying or categorizing emotions in ways that reduce them to easily digestible labels. Once emotions are labeled, analyzed, and theorized, they often become objects of intervention. This can lead to unintended consequences, such as prompting teachers to consciously curate their emotional displays based on research findings. For example, if research models how social media teachers navigate emotion labor – such as by maintaining positivity, performing engagement, or managing online criticism – it may inadvertently encourage teachers to regulate their emotional expressions to align with perceived "best practices." While this emotional regulation is not in itself problematic, if teachers focus only on adopting institutionally preferred emotions and emotional displays, they may fail to engage in reflection on why such emotions are preferred or to consider the effects of particular forms of emotion management on their identities and professional positionality.

Research on LTE also risks perpetuating its own politics of emotions (Ahmed, 2004), where emotions are socially, culturally, and politically constructed, regulated, and deployed to reinforce or challenge power structures by validating or privileging certain emotions over others, often through incorporating normative or institutional viewpoints. In this way, the research itself can create feeling rules, imposing normative expectations on how emotions should be performed (Benesch & Prior, 2023). In building on researchers' normalized perspectives, the research could unintentionally reinforce existing power structures or marginalize alternative emotional experiences. This raises critical questions: Whose emotions are being valued, and whose interests does the research serve? (Benesch & Prior, 2023). These ethical challenges call for critical reflection on how LTE research both constructs and mediates emotional norms, underscoring the need for careful, nuanced approaches to studying and representing emotions in language education.

Additionally, the concept of the politics of evidence (Denzin & Giardina, 2008) – the ways in which evidence is constructed, legitimized, and used in research and policymaking – introduces another layer of complexity to LTE research. Emotions are inherently subjective, descriptive, and often vague or ambivalent, making them vulnerable to arbitrary categorization or oversimplification in the research process. This raises a crucial ethical question: How hard are we as researchers pursuing data and at what cost? The ethical dilemma lies in what is considered meaningful evidence and how we go about obtaining it. Are we searching for deeper, more nuanced insights into emotions, or merely identifying emotions that fit within a recognizable framework to avoid any conflicts? Is it ethically justifiable to "disturb" or "induce" participants' emotional experiences, specifically difficult emotions, in pursuit of deeper data, particularly when teacher participants may be reluctant to disclose certain aspects of their emotional lives? If participants choose not to share, should we accept surface-level emotions, or do we risk imposing predefined emotional categories that align with our research agendas?

These dilemmas underscore the broader question of how evidence is constructed, legitimized, and represented in LTE research. What types of emotions do we prioritize as valid data? Do we privilege those that are easily measurable and nameable, or do we engage with the complexities and contradictions that are part of human emotions? Furthermore, how does the selection and interpretation of evidence ultimately construct the narrative of our findings? Addressing these concerns requires critical ethical reflexivity in LTE research, recognizing that the pursuit of emotional data is never neutral. The choices researchers make – whether in defining emotions, interpreting their significance, or deciding what counts as valid evidence – carry implications not only for the research process but also for how emotions in language education are understood, valued, and even regulated.

The final ethical question is: Where do researchers' responsibilities to the researched end? The meaning of ethical research varies. For some, ethical research means establishing rules that define what researchers can and cannot do in the process of knowledge building; for others, it constitutes the very rationale of research itself, where the primary task is the promotion of social justice (Hammersley, 1999). That is, ethics can extend beyond merely avoiding harm and protecting participants' rights to actively considering how research can bring about positive change for the research participants. The transformative role of research in the lives of marginalized individuals is, therefore, a fundamental ethical concern, particularly within critical research.

From post-structural and critical perspectives, emotions are not merely personal experiences but reflections of power inequalities and social structures (Ahmed, 2004; Benesch, 2017; Boler, 1999). In this view, research on LTE can examine how systemic inequalities in schools unequally affect language teachers' emotional experiences and wellbeing. Teachers often face challenging working conditions and associated emotional struggles, yet they frequently lack the power to influence these conditions. In attempting to explore these teachers' lives and emotions, researchers may, often unknowingly, assume the authority to define and evaluate their experiences (Freire, 2017). This can lead to framing these experiences in deficit terms (Canagarajah & Stanley, 2015) – not out of intent, but as a result of researchers' implicit biases and normative assumptions that fail to fully account for the complexities of these teachers' lived realities. In such a context, is it ethical for research to focus solely on theorizing LTE without translating this knowledge into meaningful contributions to improve teachers' lives and work?

Without this translation, research risks becoming extractive, serving the interests of theory and academia rather than the individuals whose experiences are being studied.

Many LTE studies have provided a wide range of direct and indirect contributions to language teachers, language learners, and our disciplinary communities, and solely extractive research is rare. However, researchers' critical reflection on these ethical pitfalls can help them recognize the power dynamics inherent in the researcher-participant relationship, the contributions of their findings, and the appropriate level of involvement in participants' lives.

Ultimately, ethical research on LTE requires more than adherence to the professional codes of ethics established by various disciplines. Researchers must engage in ongoing reflection on the ethical principles that guide their research process and ensure that these principles align with the goals of their work. This involves interrogating their own roles in mediating emotions and considering how their research influences participants, findings, and broader societal narratives. It also requires recognizing the potential for research to inadvertently create hierarchies of emotions, reinforce normative emotional standards, or prioritize certain viewpoints over others.

These ethical considerations may seem daunting and may leave us, as researchers, feeling vulnerable. However, we believe that embracing this vulnerability – rather than relying on certainty – can help us confront ethical challenges more appropriately and foster a heightened ethical sensitivity in our work.

5.3 Directions for Further Research

As of the writing of this Element, research on LTE continues to expand, with various thematic collections highlighting its significance in language education. These include LTE in relation to race, language ideologies, technology – particularly AI, online language education, and language teacher education practices, among other areas. Additionally, the recent 60th-anniversary issue of *TESOL Quarterly*, which is published every ten years as a milestone reflection on the field, features a review on *Emotion and Language Education* (Miller & Song, forthcoming). This inclusion further underscores the growing recognition of emotions as a significant area of research in language education, particularly over the past decade or so.

Despite increasing attention to LTE, several areas remain underexplored. One significant gap concerns LTE in intercultural contexts, where teachers navigate multiple, and sometimes conflicting, emotional expectations. Future research could investigate how individual teachers express and manage emotions when working across different cultural contexts. Specifically, questions arise regarding whose cultural norms or feeling rules (Hochschild, 1983) teachers adhere to, how those norms are negotiated, and in what ways they contribute to teachers' professional identities. Additionally, research could examine the extent to which feeling rules enforce or excuse particular emotional expressions in different settings, particularly among language teachers with diverse social and linguistic identities. For example, in the context of teaching English to non-native speakers, foreign teachers or native English speakers may be granted more flexibility in adhering to local norms, whereas local English teachers may be expected to comply with these norms more strictly. The varying degrees of emotion management demands may highlight the intersection of power, social identity, and emotions in language education, ultimately contributing to unequal emotional experiences (Song, 2025b).

Similarly, within the framework of emotional literacy, research could explore how language teachers re-develop or are re-socialized into emotional literacy when they cross cultural and linguistic boundaries or transition into different institutional settings. It would also be valuable to examine whether language-specific emotional norms exist and, if so, how language teachers negotiate these norms or engage in 'trans-emotioning' practices – adjusting the degree and appropriateness of emotional expressions – when teaching different languages. Research has already examined bilinguals' expressions of emotions in different languages in relation to bilingual identities (see Pavlenko, 2006). Investigating how language teachers engage with emotional literacy and feeling rules specific to each language, and how these intersect with their identities in educational contexts, would provide additional valuable insights.

Another important aspect of emotional experiences is how they are interpreted and understood. Further research could examine the dynamic relationship between LTE and student interactions. How do teachers' empathetic connections – mutual understanding of emotions and relevant norms – with students influence their emotional expression and regulation? More specifically, how do teachers' perceptions of their connection with students (e.g. whether students share similar or different cultural and linguistic backgrounds) guide the ways they express and manage certain emotions in the classroom? Additionally, how do these emotional exchanges impact teachers' ability to build relationships and maintain professional boundaries?

We also see a need for future studies to incorporate perspectives from other stakeholders in the institutional contexts where language teachers work. These might include their immediate supervisors, program staff members, or more "distant" administrators. Understanding these stakeholders' efforts (or the lack of such efforts) to support the wellbeing of language teachers is necessary for considering what teachers themselves can do. We agree with Benesch and Prior (2023, p. 7), who have argued that more research needs to turn its gaze from teachers and students to the "emotional context of educational institutions." This expanded focus can allow researchers to identify ways that institutions can change in becoming more emotionally hospitable spaces, rather than suggest that responsibility for change should always be shouldered by individual teachers.

Another important direction for research involves examining how emotions are shared in teacher education across cultural contexts. For instance, how do language teachers from diverse linguistic and cultural backgrounds communicate and interpret emotions in professional development programs? What role does cultural context play in forming teachers' perceptions of wellbeing, and how do institutional structures influence these perceptions through teacher education practices?

Finally, an emerging intersection for future research involves the interplay between psycho-cognitive and critical approaches to teacher emotions. Studies could explore how constructs such as emotional intelligence and emotional literacy or relevant pedagogical practices contribute to – or hinder – teachers' development of critical emotional reflexivity. Conversely, it would also be valuable to examine how a critical perspective on emotions influences the ways in which teachers develop and apply emotional literacy in practice. This line of inquiry could further be extended to pedagogical frameworks, investigating how language teacher education programs can integrate psycho-cognitive with critical approaches through a series of structured teaching practices for TLs' professional development.

Expanding the research agenda in LTE requires a more nuanced exploration of how emotions function within diverse teaching and learning contexts. A multidimensional approach – one that integrates individual, cultural, institutional, pedagogical dimensions – would provide a more comprehensive understanding of LTE. Simultaneously, an intersectional perspective that situates emotions within broader social and structural factors, rather than viewing them as isolated phenomena, can yield deeper insights into the complexities of LTE and its implications for practice.

References

Acheson, K., Taylor, J., & Luna, K. (2016). The burnout spiral: The emotion labor of five rural U.S. foreign language teachers. *The Modern Language Journal*, 100, 522–537. https://doi.org/10.1111/modl.12333.

Adams, T., Jones, S. L. H., & Ellis, C. (2015). *Autoethnography: Understanding Qualitative Research*. Oxford: Oxford University Press.

Ahmed, S. (2004). *The Cultural Politics of Emotion*. Edinburgh: Edinburgh University Press.

Amory, M. D. & Johnson, K. E. (2023). Provoking novice teacher development: Cognition-and-emotion in learning-to-teach. *System*, 117, 103112.

Arnold, J. & Brown, H. D. (1999). A map of the terrain. In J. Arnold (ed.), *Affect in Language Learning*. Cambridge: Cambridge University Press, pp. 1–24.

Barcelos, A. M. F. (2015). Unveiling the relationship between language learning beliefs, emotions and identities. *Studies in Second Language Learning and Teaching*, 5(2), 301–325.

Barcelos, A. M. F. (2020). Revolutionary love and peace in the construction of an English teacher's professional identity. In R. Oxford, M. Olivero, M. Harrison, and T. Gregersen (eds.), *Peacebuilding in Language Education*. Bristol: Multilingual Matters, pp. 96–109.

Barcelos, A. M. F. (2025). Pedagogical love in language teaching education: A synthesis of research. In E. Vanderheiden, C.-H. Mayer, and A. M. F. Barcelos (eds.), *Pedagogical Love in Adult Education: New Perspectives in Nurturing, Growth and Transformation*. Cham: Springer, pp. 265–284.

Barcelos, A. M. F., Aragão, R. C., Ruohotie-Lyhty, M., & Gomes, G. D. S. C. (2022). Contemporary perspectives on research about emotions in language teaching. *Revista Brasileira de Linguística Aplicada*, 22(1), 1–16.

Barcelos, A. M. F. & Coelho, H. S. H. (2016). Language learning and teaching: What's love got to do with it? In P. D. MacIntyre, T. Gregersen, and S. Mercer (eds.), *Positive Psychology in SLA*. Bristol: Multilingual Matters, pp. 130–144.

Barcelos, A. M. F. & Kalaja, P. (2011). Introduction to beliefs about SLA revisited. *System*, 39(3), 281–289.

Barcelos, A. M. F. & Ruohotie-Lyhty, M. (2018). Teachers' emotions and beliefs in second language teaching: Implications for teacher education. In J. de Dios Martínez Agudo (ed.), *Emotions in Second Language Teaching: Theory, Research and Teacher Education*. Cham: Springer, pp. 109–124.

Barcelos, A. M. F. & Ruohotie-Lyhty, M. (2023). "In teacher work you must understand others and have empathy for them!": Brazilian and Finnish language teachers' emotions and beliefs about teaching. *Apples: Journal of Applied Language Studies*, 17(2), 73–90.

Barkhuizen, G. (2016). Narrative approaches to exploring language, identity and power in language teacher education. *RELC Journal*, 47(1), 25–42.

Beck, U., Giddens, A., & Lash, S. (1994). *Reflexive Modernization: Politics, Tradition and Aesthetics in the Modern Social Order.* Cambridge: Polity Press

Benesch, S. (2012). *Considering Emotions in Critical English Language Teaching: Theories and Praxis.* New York: Routledge.

Benesch, S. (2017). *Emotions and English Language Teaching: Exploring Teachers' Emotion Labor.* New York: Routledge.

Benesch, S. (2018). Emotions as agency: Feeling rules, emotion labor, and English language teachers' decision-making. *System*, 79, 60–69.

Benesch, S. (2020). Emotions and activism: English language teachers' emotion labor as responses to institutional power. *Critical Inquiry in Language Studies*, 17(1), 26–41.

Benesch, S. & Prior, M. T. (2023). Rescuing "emotion labor" from (and for) language teacher emotion research. *System*, 113, 102995.

Bielak, J. & Mystkowska-Wiertelak, A. (2022). Language teachers' interpersonal learner-directed emotion-regulation strategies. *Language Teaching Research*, 26(6), 1082–1105.

Block, D. (2003). *The Social Turn in Second Language Acquisition.* Edinburgh: Edinburgh University Press.

Block, D. (2007). The rise of identity in SLA research, post Firth and Wagner (1997). *The Modern Language Journal*, 91(Focus Issue), 863–876.

Boler, M. (1999). *Feeling Power: Emotions and Education.* New York: Routledge.

Boler, M. & Zembylas, M. (2003). Discomforting truths: The emotional terrain of understanding differences. In P. Trifonas (ed.), *Pedagogies of Difference: Rethinking Education for Social Justice.* New York: Routledge, pp. 110–136.

Bourdieu, P. (1986). The forms of capital. In J. Richardson (ed.), *Handbook of Theory and Research for the Sociology of Education.* New York: Greenwood, pp. 241–258.

Brantmeier, E. J. (2013). Pedagogy of vulnerability: Definitions, assumptions, and applications. In J Lin, R. L. Oxford, and E. J. Brantmeier (eds.), *Re-envisioning Higher Education: Embodied Pathways to Wisdom and Social Transformation.* Charlotte, NC: Information Age, pp. 95–106.

Burns, A., Freeman, D., & Edwards, E. (2015). Theorizing and studying the language-teaching mind: Mapping research on language teacher cognition. *The Modern Language Journal*, 99(3), 585–601.

Cabiles, B. M. (2021). Towards a pedagogy of discomfort in culturally and linguistically diverse classrooms. *International Education Journal: Comparative Perspectives*, 20(2), 23–38.

Canagarajah, A. S. (2012). Teacher development in a global profession: An autoethnography. *TESOL Quarterly*, 46, 258–279.

Canagarajah, S. & P. Stanley. (2015). Ethical considerations in language policy research. In F. M. Hult and D. Cassels Johnson (eds.), *Research Methods in Language Policy and Planning: A Practical Guide*. Hoboken, NJ: Wiley, pp. 33–44.

Chabot, S. (2008). Love and revolution. *Critical Sociology*, 34(6), 803–828.

Chang, H. (2008). *Autoethnography as Method*. Walnut Creek, CA: Left Coast Press.

Chen, Z., Sun, Y., & Jia, Z. (2022). A study of student-teachers' emotional experiences and their development of professional identities. *Frontiers of Psychology*, 12, 810146.

Cowie, N. (2011). Emotions that experienced English as a foreign language (EFL) teachers feel about their students, their colleagues and their work. *Teaching and Teacher Education*, 27(1), 235–242.

Cutri, R. M. & Whiting, E. F. (2015). The emotional work of discomfort and vulnerability in multicultural teacher education. *Teachers and Teaching*, 21(8), 1010–1025.

De Costa, P. I. & Nazari, M. (eds.) (forthcoming). *Language Teacher Educator Emotions*. Cambridge: Cambridge University Press.

De Costa, P. I. & Norton, B. (2017). Introduction: Identity, transdisciplinarity, and the good language teacher. *The Modern Language Journal*, 101(S1), 3–14.

De Dios Martínez Agudo, J. (ed.) (2018). *Emotions in Second Language Teaching: Theory, Research and Teacher Education*. Cham: Springer.

de Oliveira, A. C. T. & Barcelos, A. M. F. (2024). Emotional labor of a Brazilian public school teacher: Domination and resistance in a neoliberal context. *International Review of Applied Linguistics in Language Teaching*, 62(3), 1237–1255.

Delgado, R. (1996). Rodrigo's eleventh chronicle: Empathy and false empathy. *California Law Review*, 84(1), 61–100.

Denzin, N. K. & Giardina, M. D. (eds.) (2008). *Qualitative Inquiry and the Politics of Evidence*. Walnut Creek, CA: Left Coast Press.

Derahkhshan, A., Greenier, V., & Fathi, J. (2023). Exploring the interplay between a loving pedagogy, creativity, and work engagement among EFL/ESL teachers: A multinational study. *Current Psychology*, 42(26), 22803–22822.

Dewaele, J. M. & Wu, A. (2021). Predicting the emotional labor strategies of Chinese English Foreign Language teachers. *System*, 103, 102660.

Dewaele, J. M., Chen, X., Padilla, A. M., & Lake, J. (2019). The flowering of positive psychology in foreign language teaching and acquisition research. *Frontiers in Psychology*, 10, 2128.

Dewaele, J. M., Gkonou, C., & Mercer, S. (2018). Do ESL/EFL teachers' emotional intelligence, teaching experience, proficiency and gender affect their classroom practice? In J. De Dios Martínez Agudo (ed.), *Emotions in Second Language Teaching: Theory, Research and Teacher Education*. Cham: Springer, pp. 125–141.

Dewey, J. (1895). The theory of emotion. *Psychological Review*, 2(1), 13.

Eraldemir-Tuyan, S. (2019). An Emotional Literacy Improvement (ELI) Program for EFL Teachers: Insiders' Views. *European Journal of Educational Research*, 8(4), 1113–1125.

Fathi, J., Greenier, V., & Derakhshan, A. (2021). Self-efficacy, reflection, and burnout among Iranian EFL teachers: The mediating role of emotion regulation. *Iranian Journal of Language Teaching Research*, 9(2), 13–37.

Feryok, A. (Ed.) (2024). *Language Teacher Identity and Wellbeing*. Bristol: Multilingual Matters.

Freire, P. (2017). *Pedagogy of the Oppressed*. (M. B. Ramos, Trans.). New York: Penguin Classics.

Freire, P. (2021). *Pedagogy of Hope: Reliving Pedagogy of the Oppressed*. (R. R. Barr, Trans.). London: Bloomsbury.

Frenzel, A. C., Daniels, L., & Burić, I. (2021). Teacher emotions in the classroom and their implications for students. *Educational Psychologist*, 56(4), 250–264.

Frenzel, A. C., Pekrun, R., Goetz, T., et al. (2016). Measuring teachers' enjoyment, anger, and anxiety: The Teacher Emotions Scales (TES). *Contemporary Educational Psychology*, 46, 148–163.

Gao, Y. & Cui, Y. (2022). Agency as power: An ecological exploration of an emerging language teacher leaders' emotional changes in an educational reform. *Frontiers in Psychology*, 13, 958260.

Gao, Y. & Cui, Y. (2023). Emotional tensions as rewards: An emerging teacher leader's identity construction in EFL textbook development. *TESOL Journal*, 14(1), 1–17.

Gao, Y., Liu, Y., Zeng, Y., & Wang, X. (2024). Studies on language teachers' beliefs and emotions: Current status and future directions. *Heliyon*, 10, e38695.

Garrison, J. (2003). Dewey's theory of emotions: The unity of thought and emotion in naturalistic functional "co-ordination" of behavior. *Transactions of the Charles S. Peirce Society*, 39(3), 405–443.

Ghanizadeh, A. & Royaei, N. (2015). Emotional facet of language teaching: Emotion regulation and emotional labor strategies as predictors of teacher burnout. *International Journal of Pedagogies and Learning*, 10(2), 139–150.

Giddens, A. (1984). *The Constitution of Society: Outline of the Theory of Structuration*. Cambridge: Polity Press.

Gkonou C. & Mercer S. (2017) *Understanding Emotional and Social Intelligence among English Language Teachers*. London: British Council.

Gkonou, C. & Miller, E. R. (2019). Caring and emotional labour: Language teachers' engagement with anxious learners in private language school classrooms. *Language Teaching Research*, 23(3), 372–387.

Gkonou, C. & Miller, E. R. (2023). Relationality in language teacher emotion regulation: Regulating emotions through, with and for others. *System*, 115, 103046.

Gkonou, C. & Miller, E. R. (2021). An exploration of language teacher reflection, emotion labor, and emotional capital. *TESOL Quarterly*, 55, 134–155.

Gkonou, C., Dewaele, J. M., & King, J. (2020). Introduction to the emotional rollercoaster of language learning. In C. Gkonou, J. M. Dewaele, and J. King (eds.), *The Emotional Rollercoaster of Language Teaching*. Bristol: Multilingual Matters, pp. 1–12.

Goetze, J. (2023). An appraisal-based examination of language teacher emotions in anxiety-provoking classroom situations using vignette methodology. *The Modern Language Journal*, 107(1), 328–352.

Golombek, P. R. (2015). Redrawing the boundaries of language teacher cognition: Language teacher educators' emotion, cognition, and activity. *Modern Language Journal*, 99(3), 470–484.

Golombek, P. R. & Doran, M. (2014). Unifying cognition, emotion, and activity in language teacher professional development. *Teaching and Teacher Education*, 39, 102–111.

Golombek, P. R. & Johnson, K. E. (2004). Narrative inquiry as a mediational space: Examining emotional and cognitive dissonance in second-language teachers' development. *Teachers and Teaching*, 10(3), 307–327.

Greenier, V., Derakhshan, A., & Fathi, J. (2021). Emotion regulation and psychological well-being in teacher work engagement: A case of British and Iranian English language teachers. *System*, 97, 102446.

Gross, J. J., Richards, J. M., & John, O. P. (2006). Emotion regulation in everyday life. In D. K. Snyder, J. A. Simpson, and J. N. Hughes (eds.), *Emotion Regulation in Couples and Families: Pathways to Dysfunction and Health*. Washington, DC: American Psychological Association, pp. 13–35.

Hammersley, M. (1999). Some reflections on the current state of qualitative research. *Research Intelligence*, 70, 16–18.

Hammersley, M. & Traianou, A. (2012). *Ethics and Educational Research*. British Educational Research Association on-line resource. www.t-rex.ie/wp-content/uploads/2017/02/BERA-Ethics-and-Educational-Research.pdf. Last accessed on February 4, 2025.

Han, J., Jin, L., & Yin, H. (2023). Mapping the research on language teacher emotion: A systematic literature review. *System*, 103138.

Han, Y., Wei, R., & Wang, J. (2023). An ecological examination of teacher emotions in an EFL context. *Frontiers in Psychology*, 14, 1058046.

Hargreaves, A. (1998). The emotional practice of teaching. *Teaching and Teacher Education*, 14(8), 835–854.

Hargreaves, A. (2001). Emotional geographies of teaching. *Teachers College Record*, 103(6), 1056–1080.

Hawkins, M. & Norton, B. (2009). Critical language teacher education. In A. Burns and J. C. Richards (eds.), *Cambridge Guide to Second Language Teacher Education*. Cambridge: Cambridge University Press, pp. 30–39.

Her, L. & De Costa, P. I. (2022). When language teacher emotions and language policy intersect: A critical perspective. *System*, 105, 102745.

Heydarnejad, T., Zareian, G., Ghaniabadi, S., & Adel, S. M. R. (2021). Measuring language teacher emotion regulation: Development and validation of the language teacher emotion regulation inventory at workplace (LTERI). *Frontiers in Psychology*, 12, 708888.

Hochschild, A. (1979). Emotion work, feeling rules, and social structures. *American Journal of Sociology*, 85(3), 551–575.

Hochschild, A. (1983). *The Managed Heart: Commercialization of Human Feelings*. Berkeley, CA: University of California Press.

Holstein, J. & Gubrium, J. (2003). Active interviewing. In J. F. Gubrium and J. A. Holstein (eds.), *Active Interviewing*. Thousand Oaks, CA: Sage, pp. 66–80.

hooks, b. (1994). *Teaching to Transgress: Education as the Practice of Freedom*. New York: Routledge.

Hulda, G. & Zhao, T. (2024). "Don't cry or show your anger in public places": Exploring the emotional labor experiences of novice Chinese language teachers in Cameroon. *Teaching and Teacher Education*, 148, 104690.

Imai, Y. (2010). Emotions in SLA: New insights from collaborative learning for an EFL classroom. *The Modern Language Journal*, 94(2), 278–292.

Imperiale, M. G., Phipps, A., Al-Masri, N., & Fassetta, G. (2017). Pedagogies of hope and resistance: English language education in the context of the Gaza

Strip, Palestine. In E. J. Erling (ed.), *English across the Fracture Lines*. British Council: London, pp. 31–38.

Isenbarger, L. & Zembylas, M. (2006). The emotional labour of caring in teaching. *Teaching and teacher education*, 22(1), 120–134.

Ji, Y., Oubibi, M., Chen, S., Yin, Y., & Zhou, Y. (2022) Pre-service teachers' emotional experience: Characteristics, dynamics and sources amid the teaching practicum. *Frontiers of Psychology*, 13, 968513.

Jin Y. X. & Dewaele J. M. (2018). The effect of positive orientation and perceived social support on foreign language classroom anxiety. *System* 74, 149–157. https://doi.org/10.1016/j.system.2018.01.002.

Johnson, K. E. & Golombek, P. R. (2011). The transformative power of narrative in second language teacher education. *TESOL Quarterly*, 45(3), 486–509.

Johnson, K. E. & Worden, D. (2014). Cognitive/emotional dissonance as growth points in learning to teach. *Language and Sociocultural Theory*, 1(2), 125–150.

Kanno, Y. & Stuart C. (2011) Learning to Become a Second Language Teacher: Identities-in-Practice. *The Modern Language Journal*, 95, 236–252.

Kaukko, M., Wilkinson, J., & Kohli, R. K. (2021). Pedagogical love in Finland and Australia: A study of refugee children and their teachers. *Pedagogy, Culture & Society*, 30(5), 731–747.

Kelchtermans, G. (2005). Teachers' emotions in educational reforms: Self-understanding, vulnerable commitment and micropolitical literacy. *Teaching and Teacher Education*, 21, 995–1006.

Kelchtermans, G. (2011). Vulnerability in teaching: The moral and political roots of a structural condition. In C. Day and J. K. Lee (eds.), *New Understandings of Teacher's Work: Emotions and Educational Change*. Dordrecht: Springer, pp. 65–82.

Khajavy, G. H., Ghonsooly, B., Fatemi, A. H., & Frenzel, A. C. (2018). Antecedents of pleasant and unpleasant emotions of EFL teachers using an appraisal-theoretical framework. *Iranian Journal of Language Teaching Research*, 6(2), 39–55.

Kim, M., Cho, E., & Kim, S. (2023). Going beyond boundaries: A collaborative autoethnographic study of three teachers' negotiation of cognitive/emotional dissonances. *Language Teaching Research*, 13621688231195317.

King, J. & Ng, K. Y. S. (2018). Teacher emotions and the emotional labour of second language teaching. In S. Mercer and A. Kostoulos (eds.), *Language Teacher Psychology*. Bristol: Multilingual Matters, pp. 141–157.

Kliueva, E. & Tsagari, D. (2018). Emotional literacy in EFL classes: The relationship between teachers' trait emotional intelligence level and the use of emotional literacy strategies. *System*, 78, 38–53.

Kocaba-Gedik, P. & Ortaçtepe Hart, D. (2021). "It's not like that at all": A poststructuralist case study on language teacher identity and emotional labor. *Journal of Language, Identity & Education*, 20(2), 103–117.

Kubanyiova, M. (2012). *Teacher Development in Action: Understanding Language Teachers' Conceptual Change*. Basingstoke: Palgrave MacMillan.

La Placa V., McNaught A., & Knight A. (2013). Discourse on wellbeing in research and practice. *International Journal of Wellbeing*, (3)1, 116–125.

Lanas, M. (2017). An argument for love in intercultural education for teacher education. *Intercultural Education*, 28(6), 557–570.

Lanas, M. & Zembylas, M. (2015). Revolutionary love at work in an arctic school with conflicts. *Teaching Education*, 26(3), 272–287.

Lantolf, J. P. (2000). Second language learning as a mediated process. *Language Teaching*, 33(2), 79–96.

Lasky, S. (2005). A sociocultural approach to understanding teacher identity, agency, and professional vulnerability in a context of secondary school reform. *Teaching and Teacher Education*, 21, 899–916.

Lazarus, R. S. (1991). Progress on a cognitive-motivational-relational theory of emotion. *American Psychologist*, 46(8), 819–834.

Li, C., Jiang, G., & Dewaele, J. M. (2018). Understanding Chinese high school students' foreign language enjoyment: Validation of the Chinese version of the foreign language enjoyment scale. *System*, 76, 183–196.

Li, D. & Zhang, L. (2023). Exploring EFL learners' cognitive/emotional dissonance in content-based foreign language instruction: An ecological perspective. *System*, 114, 103019.

Li, J. & De Costa, P. I. (2023). "Small" language teacher emotions between nationalism and neoliberalism. *System*, 116, 103071.

Li, L., Curdt-Christiansen, X. L., & Zhu, D. (2024). Becoming and being a teacher through emotion discourse: A case study of a novice EMI teacher. *Journal of Multilingual and Multicultural Development*, 1–14.

Li, W. & Rawal, H. (2018). Waning and waxing of love: Unpacking layers of teacher emotion. *Chinese Journal of Applied Linguistics*, 41(4), 552–570.

MacIntyre, P. D., Gregersen, T., & Mercer, S. (2020). Language teachers' coping strategies during the Covid-19 conversion to online teaching: Correlations with stress, wellbeing and negative emotions. *System*, 94, 102352.

MacIntyre, P. D., Ross, J., Talbot, K., et al. (2019). Stressors, personality and wellbeing among language teachers. *System*, 82, 26–38.

Martínez Agudo, J. D. D. (2024). The power of subjectivity in CLIL assessment: Evidence of cognitive/emotional dissonance. *Journal of Multilingual and Multicultural Development*, 1–16.

May, T. & Perry, B. (2014). Reflexivity and the practice of qualitative research. In U. Flick (ed.), *Reflexivity and the Practice of Qualitative Research*. Thousand Oaks, CA: Sage, pp.109–122.

Mercer, S. (2011). Language learner self-concept: Complexity, continuity and change. *System*, 39(3), 335–346.

Mercer, S. (2021). An agenda for well-being in ELT: An ecological perspective. *ELT Journal*, 75(1), 14–21.

Mercer, S. (2023). The wellbeing of language teachers in the private sector: An ecological perspective. *Language Teaching Research*, 27(5), 1054–1077.

Mercer, S. & Murillo-Miranda, C. (2025). Research agenda on well-being and language education. *Language Teaching*, 58, 377–395.

Mercer, S., Oberdorfer, P., & Saleem, M. (2016). Helping language teachers to thrive: Using positive psychology to promote teachers' professional well-being. In D. Gabryś and D. Gałajda (eds.), *Positive Psychology Perspectives on Foreign Language Learning and Teaching*. Cham: Springer, pp. 213–229.

Miller, E. R. & Gkonou, C. (2018). Language teacher agency, emotion labor and emotional rewards in tertiary-level English language programs. *System*, 79, 49–59.

Miller, E. R. & Gkonou, C. (2023). Exploring teacher caring as a "happy object" in language teacher accounts of happiness. *Applied Linguistics*, 44(2), 328–346.

Miller, E. R. & Gkonou, C. (2024). Investigating entanglements in experienced language teachers' sense of belonging and what belonging does. *International Journal of Applied Linguistics*, 1–10.

Miller, E. R. & Song, J. (forthcoming). Emotion and language education. *TESOL Quarterly*.

Morgan, B. (2004). Teacher identity as pedagogy: Towards a field-internal conceptualisation in bilingual and second language education. *International Journal of Bilingual Education and Bilingualism*, 7(2–3), 172–188.

Morris, S. (2022). Performing motivating and caring identities: Identity and the emotions of non-Japanese university teachers of English. In M. Mielick, R. Kubota, and L. Lawrence (eds.), *Discourses of Identity: Language Learning, Teaching and Reclamation Perspectives in Japan*. Cham: Palgrave, pp. 341–358.

Morris, S. (2025). *Language Teacher Emotion Regulation: An Exploration in Japan*. Bristol: Multilingual Matters.

Morris, S. & King, J. (2018). Teacher frustration and emotion regulation in university language teaching. *Chinese Journal of Applied Linguistics*, 41(4), 433–452.

Morris, S. & King, J. (2020). Emotion regulation among university EFL teachers in Japan: The dynamic interplay between context and emotional behaviour. In

C. Gkonou, J. M. Dewaele, and J. King (eds.), *The Emotional Rollercoaster of Language Teaching*. Bristol: Multilingual Matters, pp. 193–210.

Morris, S. & King, J. (2023). University language teachers' contextually dependent uses of instrumental emotion regulation. *System*, 116, 103080.

Morris, S. & King, J. (2024). Language teacher emotions: A systematic review. In Z. Tajeddin and T.S.C. Farrell (eds.), *Handbook of Language Teacher Education: Critical Review and Research Synthesis*. Cham: Springer, pp. 1–27.

Moskowitz, S. & Dewaele, J. M. (2019). Is teacher happiness contagious? A study of the link between perceptions of language teacher happiness and student attitudes. *Innovation in Language Learning and Teaching*, 15(2), 117–130.

Mosqueda, H. C. (2025). The Role of Emotions in Teacher Agency: A Study of Mexican English Language Educators. *Profile: Issues in Teachers' Professional Development*, 27(1), 67–82.

Mystkowska-Wiertelak, A. (2022). Teachers' accounts of learners' engagement and disaffection in the language classroom. *The Language Learning Journal*, 50(3), 393–405.

Nazari, M. & De Costa, P. I. (2024). EMI teachers' emotion labour: capturing classroom, institutional and sociocultural ecologies. *Journal of Multilingual and Multicultural Development*, 1–14.

Nazari, M. & Hu, G. (2024). Novice language teachers steer their emotional vulnerabilities toward exercising agency: A dialogical-community of practice study. *Teaching and Teacher Education*, 152.

Nazari, M. & Kamali, J. (2024). An ecological inquiry into transnational English language teachers' emotional vulnerability and agency. *British Journal of Educational Studies*, 73(1), 97–118.

Nazari, M. & Molana, K. (2023). "Predators of Emotions": The Role of School Assessment Policies in English Language Teachers' Emotion Labor. *TESOL Quarterly*, 57, 1226–1255.

Nazari, M., Karimi, M. N., & De Costa, P. I. (2023). Emotion and identity construction in teachers of young learners of English: An ecological perspective. *System*, 112, 102972.

Nazari, M., Keshvari, Z., & Hu, G. (2024). Contributions of an emotion-oriented professional development course to the ecology of language teacher agency. *System*, 127, 103542.

Nazari, M., Keshvari, Z., & Hu, G. (2025). Professional learning community as a site for addressing emotional tensions: Contributions to language teacher identity (re)construction. *British Journal of Educational Studies*, 1–24.

Nejadghanbar, H., Song, J., & Hu, G. (2024). English language teachers' emotional vulnerability in the era of self-branding on social media. *TESOL Quarterly*, 58(4), 1734–1760.

Nguyen, M. H. (2014). Preservice EAL teaching as emotional experiences: Practicum experience in an Australian secondary school. *Australian Journal of Teacher Education*, 39(8), 63–84.

Nikoopour, J., Farsani, M. A., Tajbakhsh, M., & Kiyaie, S. H. S. (2012). The relationship between trait emotional intelligence and self-efficacy among Iranian EFL teachers. *Journal of Language Teaching and Research*, 3(6), 1165.

Norton, B. (2000). *Identity and Language Learning: Gender, Ethnicity, and Educational Change*. New York: Longman.

Ohito, E. O. (2016). Making the emperor's new clothes visible in anti-racist teacher education: Enacting a pedagogy of discomfort with white preservice teachers. *Equity & Excellence in Education*, 49(4), 454–467.

Oxford, R. (2015). Emotion as the amplifier and the primary motive: Some theories of emotion with relevance to language learning. *Studies in Second Language Learning and Teaching*, 5(3), 371–393.

Oxford, R. L. (1995). When emotion meets (meta) cognition in language learning histories. *International Journal of Educational Research*, 23(7), 581–594.

Pavlenko A. (2013). The affective turn in SLA: From "affective factors" to "language desire" and "commodification of affect." In D. Gabrys-Barker and J. Bielska (eds.), *The Affective Dimension in Second Language Acquisition*. Bristol: Multilingual Matters, pp. 3–28.

Pavlenko, A. (ed.) (2006). *Bilingual Minds: Emotional Experience, Expression, and Representation*. Bristol: Multilingual Matters.

Pereira, A. J. (2018). Caring to teach: Exploring the affective economies of English teachers in Singapore. *Chinese Journal of Applied Linguistics*, 41(4), 488–505.

Petrides, K.V. (2009). Psychometric properties of the trait emotional intelligence questionnaire (TEIQue). In J. Parker, D. Saklofske, and C. Stough (eds.), *Assessing Emotional Intelligence*. Boston, MA: Springer, pp. 85–101.

Pinner, R. (2019). *Authenticity and Teacher-Student Motivational Synergy: A Narrative of Language Teaching*. New York: Routledge.

Poehner, M. E. & Lantolf, J. P. (2024). *Sociocultural Theory and Second Language Developmental Education*. Cambridge: Cambridge University Press.

Porto, M. & Zembylas, M. (2024). Pedagogies of discomfort in the world language classroom: Ethical tensions and considerations for educators. *The Modern Language Journal*, 108(2), 412–429.

Prior, M. T. (2019). Elephants in the room: An "affective turn," or just feeling our way? *The Modern Language Journal*, 103(2), 516–527.

Rezai, A., Namaziandost, E., & Teo, T. (2024). EFL teachers' perceptions of emotional literacy: A phenomenological investigation in Iran. *Teaching and Teacher Education*, 140, 104486.

Richards, J. C. (2022). Exploring emotions in language teaching. *RELC Journal*, 53(1), 225–239.

Rodrigues, N. N. (2015). *Relationships between pre-service teachers' emotions and beliefs about learning and teaching English*. Unpublished Ph. D. Dissertation. Viçosa, Universidade Federal de Viçosa, Brasil.

Sah, P. K. (2023). Emotion and imagination in English-medium instruction programs: Illuminating its dark side through Nepali students' narratives. *Linguistics and Education*, 75, 101150.

Scheffler, I. (1977). In praise of the cognitive emotions. *Teachers College Record*, 79(2), 1–10.

Seligman, M. E. P. & Csikszentmihalyi, M. (2000). Positive psychology: An introduction. *American Psychologist*, 55(1), 5–14.

Sembiante, S. F. & Tian, Z. (2023). Translanguaging: A pedagogy of heteroglossic hope. *International Journal of Bilingual Education and Bilingualism*, 26(8), 919–923.

Seydi Shahivand, E. & Moradkhani, S. (2020). The relationship between EFL teachers' trait emotional intelligence and reflective practices: A structural equation modeling approach. *Innovation in Language Learning and Teaching*, 14(5), 466–480.

Shen, G. (2022). Anxiety, boredom, and burnout among EFL teachers: the mediating role of emotion regulation. *Frontiers in Psychology*, 13, 842920.

Simons, M. & Smits, T. (Eds.). (2020). *Language Education and Emotions: Research into Emotions and Language Learners, Language Teachers and Educational Processes*. New York: Routledge.

Smirnova, L. (2023). Teachers' motives, agency and Vygotsky's notion of perezhivanie. *European Journal of Applied Linguistics and TEFL*, 12(1), 173–189.

Smith, L. & King, J. (2018). Silence in the foreign language classroom: The emotional challenges for L2 teachers. In J. Martínez Agudo (ed.), *Emotions in Second Language Teaching*. Springer, pp. 323–340.

Song, J. (2016). Emotions and language teacher identity: Conflicts, vulnerability, and transformation. *TESOL Quarterly*, 50(3), 631–654.

Song, J. (2018). Critical approaches to emotions of non-native English speaking teachers. *Chinese Journal of Applied Linguistics*, 41(4), 453–467.

Song, J. (2021). Emotional labour and professional development in ELT. *ELT Journal*, 75(4), 482–492.

Song, J. (2022). The emotional landscape of online teaching: An autoethnographic exploration of vulnerability and emotional reflexivity. *System*, 106, 102774.

Song, J. (2023). Korean language teachers' vulnerability about English competency in Korean-only classrooms. *Asian Pacific Journal of Second and Foreign Language Education*, 8(16), 1–19.

Song, J. (2025a). Pedagogizing teacher emotions for empowering language teachers: Emotion as critical inquiry in language teacher education. *RELC Journal*, 56(1), 138–150.

Song, J. (2025b). Who has the right to express frustration? Uneven emotion labor among students in an EMI classroom. *International Journal of Applied Linguistics*, 1–11.

Song, J. (2025c). Advocating for NNESTs' emotional resistance towards inequality. In H. Uysal and H. Kim (eds.), *Criticality, Agency, and Language Teacher Identities: Research and Praxis from Global Teacher Education*. London: Bloomsbury, pp. 97–114.

Song, J. & Nejadghanbar, H. (2024). Consumerist discourses on social media and language teacher educator identity tensions. *TESOL Journal*, 1–17.

Song, J. & Olazabal-Arias, W. (2024). Feeling power in collaborative discourse. In Z. Tajeddin and B. Yazan (eds.), *Language Teacher Identity Tensions: Nexus of Agency, Emotion, and Investment*. New York: Routledge, pp. 246–260.

Song, J. & Park, J. S. Y. (2019). The politics of emotions in ELT: Structure of feeling and anxiety of Korean English teachers. *Changing English*, 26(3), 252–262.

Song, J. & Valentine, B. (2024). Emotion labor in teacher collaboration emotion labor: Towards Developing Emotional Reflexivity. *International Review of Applied Linguistics and Language Teaching*, 62(3), 1191–1212.

Song, J. & Wu, A. E. (2024). Intergenerational autoethnography of heritage language maintenance: Focusing on emotion, identity, and power. *The Modern Language Journal*, 108(S1), 14–36.

Stevenson, M. (2024). Understanding the emotional labor of English language teaching while Black in the United States. *TESOL Quarterly*, 58(4), 1347–1371.

Sulis, G., Mairitsch, A., Babić, S., et al. (2022). Language teacher wellbeing and psychological capital. *Konińskie Studia Językowe*, 10(2), 22.

Sun, L. (2023). Pedagogies of discomfort and empathy in foreign language education: Fostering EFL learners' critical global thinking through literature and art. *Thinking Skills and Creativity*, 50, 101411.

Swain, M. (2013). The inseparability of cognition and emotion in second language learning. *Language Teaching*, 46(2), 195–207.

Tajeddin, Z. & Keshvari, Z. (2025). Emotional tensions in identity transition from teachers to teacher educators: Voices from early-career teacher educators. *Asian-Pacific Journal of Second and Foreign Language Education*, 10(1), 1–18.

Tajeddin, Z. & Yazan, B. (Eds.). (2024). *Language Teacher Identity Tensions: Nexus of Agency, Emotion, and Investment*. New York: Taylor & Francis.

Talbot, K. & Mercer, S. (2018). Exploring university ESL/EFL teachers' emotional well-being and emotional regulation in the United States, Japan and Austria. *Chinese Journal of Applied Linguistics*, 41(4), 410–432.

Tao, J., Yuetling, X., Wang, S., & Gao, X. (Forthcoming). The emotions of language teachers: A systematic review of studies from 2015 to 2024. *Language Teaching*.

Teng, F. (2017). Emotional development and construction of teacher identity: Narrative interactions about the pre-service teachers' practicum experiences. *Australian Journal of Teacher Education*, 42(11), 117–134.

Toker-Bradshaw, Ş. & Tezgiden-Cakcak, Y. (2024). Emotion-identity-agency triangle in practicum experience: A pre-service second language teacher's development of critical emotional reflexivity. *RELC Journal*, 56(1), 50–65.

Uştuk, Ö. & Yazan, B. (2024). Tensions in an identity-oriented language teaching practicum: A dialogic approach. *TESOL Quarterly*, 58(1), 363–393.

Vega, H. & Fallas-Escobar, C. (2022). Language teacher candidates' emotion labor: Transcending circulating language ideologies. In G. Martínez-Alba, L. J. Pentón-Herrera, and E. Trinh (eds.), *Teacher Well-being in English Language Teaching*. New York: Routledge, pp. 189–206.

Vitanova, G. (2024). "It's just a feeling!": Emotions and intersectionality in language teacher narratives. *TESOL Quarterly*, 58(4), 1493–1517.

Vygotsky, L. S. (1978). *Mind in Society: The Development of Higher Psychological Processes*. Cambridge, MA: Harvard University Press.

Wang, Y., Derakhshan, A., & Pan, Z. (2022). Positioning an agenda on a loving pedagogy in second language acquisition: Conceptualization, practice, and research. *Frontiers in Psychology*, 13(2), 894190.

Warren, C. A. (2015). Conflicts and contradictions: Conceptions of empathy and the work of good-intentioned White female teachers. *Urban Education*, 50(5), 572–600.

Warner, C. & Diao, W. (2022). Caring is pedagogy: Foreign language teachers' emotion labor in crisis. *Linguistics and Education*, 71, 101100.

White, C. J. (2018). The emotional turn in applied linguistics and TESOL: Significance, challenges and prospects. In J. de Dios Martínez Agudo (ed.),

Emotions in Second Language Teaching: Theory, Research and Teacher Education. Cham: Springer, pp. 19–34.

Wolff, D. & De Costa, P. I. (2017). Expanding the language teacher identity landscape: An investigation of the emotions and strategies of a NNEST. *The Modern Language Journal*, 101(S1), 76–90.

Xiyun, S., Fathi, J., Shirbagi, N., & Mohammaddokht, F. (2022). A structural model of teacher self-efficacy, emotion regulation, and psychological well-being among English teachers. *Frontiers in Psychology*, 13, 904151.

Xu, H. (2024). *Language Teachers' Social Cognition*. Cambridge, MA: Cambridge University Press.

Yang, S. & Sato, M. (Forthcoming). Language teacher emotion. *Language Teaching*.

Yang, S., Shu, D., & Yin, H. (2022). The bright side of dark emotions: Exploring EFL teachers' emotions, emotional capital, and engagement in curriculum implementation. *Teaching and Teacher Education*, 117, 103811.

Yazan, B. (2019). Identities and ideologies in a language teacher candidate's autoethnography: Making meaning of storied experience. *TESOL Journal*, 10(4), 1–21.

Yazan, B. (2023). Incorporating teacher emotions and identity in teacher education practices: Affordances of critical autoethnographic narrative. *The Language Learning Journal*, 51(5), 649–661.

Yazan, B. (2024). *Autoethnography in Language Education: Tensions, Characteristics, and Methods*. Cham: Palgrave.

Yazan, B. (2025). Emotional entanglements and intersectional language teacher identities in critical autoethnographic narratives. *International Journal of Applied Linguistics*, 1–12. https://doi.org/10.1111/ijal.12697.

Yuan, R. & Lee, I. (2014). The cognitive, social and emotional processes of teacher identity construction in a pre-service teacher education programme. *Research Papers in Education*, 30(4), 469–491.

Zaidi, R., Strong, T., Oliver, C., Alwarraq, H., & Naqvi, A. (2021). The understated role of pedagogical love and human emotion in refugee education. *International Journal of Qualitative Studies in Education*, 35(6), 678–696.

Zhang, Y. & Zhang, L. J. (2024). "Good for me to leave it for good": A longitudinal study on how emotion labor in teaching contributes to a beginning EFL teacher's resignation. *TESOL Quarterly*, 58(4), 1460–1492.

Zayas-Santiago, C. & Smith, S. A. (2024). "I am not *that* teacher": Latinx teachers' linguacultural experiences and transformative practices as resources for hope. *Pedagogies: An International Journal*, 20(1), 120–142.

Zembylas, M. (2003). Emotions and teacher identity: A poststructural perspective. *Teachers and Teaching*, 9(3), 213–238.

Zembylas, M. (2005). Discursive practices, genealogies, and emotional Rules: A poststructuralist view on emotion and identity in teaching. *Teaching and Teacher Education*, 21(8), 935–948.

Zembylas, M. (2007). Emotional capital and education: Theoretical insights from Bourdieu. *British Journal of Educational Studies*, 55, 443–463.

Zembylas, M. (2008). Engaging with issues of cultural diversity and discrimination through critical emotional reflexivity in online learning. *Adult Education Quarterly*, 59(1), 61–82.

Zembylas, M. (2012). Pedagogies of strategic empathy: Navigating through the emotional complexities of anti-racism in higher education. *Teaching in Higher education*, 17(2), 113–125.

Zembylas, M. (2014). The place of emotion in teacher reflection: Elias, Foucault and "critical emotional reflexivity." *Power and Education*, 6(2), 210–222. 17516492632.

Zembylas, M. (2017). Love as ethico-political practice: Inventing reparative pedagogies of aimance in "disjointed" times. *Journal of Curriculum and Pedagogy*, 14(1), 23–38.

Zembylas, M. & McGlynn, C. (2012). Discomforting pedagogies: Emotional tensions, ethical dilemmas and transformative possibilities. *British Educational Research Journal*, 38(1), 41–59.

Zembylas, M. & Papamichael, E. (2017). Pedagogies of discomfort and empathy in multicultural teacher education. *Intercultural Education*, 28(1), 1–19.

Zhang, X. (2021). The effect of English as a foreign language teachers' optimism and affectivity on their psychological well-being. *Frontiers in Psychology*, 12, 816204.

Zhang, Y. & Yusof, F. M. (2024). Exploring emotional experiences of Chinese university novice EFL teachers: An ecological perspective. *Acta Psychologica*, 251, 104590.

Zhang, Y., Lantolf, J. P., & Meng, Y. (2022). The emotion-intellect dialectic in an EFL teacher's development of a research identity: A sociocultural perspective. *System*, 111, 102954.

Zhi, R. & Wang, Y. (2023). English as a foreign language teachers' professional success, loving pedagogy and creativity: A structural equation modeling approach. *Thinking Skills and Creativity*, 49, 101370.

Cambridge Elements

Language Teaching

Heath Rose
University of Oxford

Heath Rose is Professor of Applied Linguistics at the University of Oxford and Deputy Director (People) of the Department of Education. Before moving into academia, Heath worked as a language teacher in Australia and Japan in both school and university contexts. He is author of numerous books, such as *Introducing Global Englishes, The Japanese Writing System, Data Collection Research Methods in Applied Linguistics,* and *Global Englishes for Language Teaching.*

Jim McKinley
University College London

Jim McKinley is Professor of Applied Linguistics at IOE Faculty of Education and Society, University College London. He has taught in higher education in the UK, Japan, Australia, and Uganda, as well as US schools. His research targets implications of globalization for L2 writing, language education, and higher education studies, particularly the teaching-research nexus and English medium instruction. Jim is co-author and co-editor of several books on research methods in applied linguistics. He is an Editor-in-Chief of the journal *System*.

Advisory Board

Gary Barkhuizen, *University of Auckland*
Marta Gonzalez-Lloret, *University of Hawaii*
Li Wei, *UCL Institute of Education*
Victoria Murphy, *University of Oxford*
Brian Paltridge, *University of Sydney*
Diane Pecorari, *Leeds University*
Christa Van der Walt, *Stellenbosch University*
Yongyan Zheng, *Fudan University*

About the Series

This Elements series aims to close the gap between researchers and practitioners by allying research with language teaching practices, in its exploration of research informed teaching, and teaching-informed research. The series builds upon a rich history of pedagogical research in its exploration of new insights within the field of language teaching.

Cambridge Elements

Language Teaching

Elements in the Series

Teaching English as an International Language
Ali Fuad Selvi, Nicola Galloway and Heath Rose

Peer Assessment in Writing Instruction
Shulin Yu

Assessment for Language Teaching
Aek Phakiti and Constant Leung

Sociocultural Theory and Second Language Developmental Education
Matthew E. Poehner and James P. Lantolf

Language Learning beyond English: Learner Motivation in the Twenty-First Century
Ursula Lanvers

Extensive Reading
Jing Zhou

Willingness to Communicate in a Second Language
Jian-E Peng

Core Concepts in English for Specific Purposes
Helen Basturkmen

Teaching Second Language Academic Writing
Christine M. Tardy

Metacognition in Language Teaching
Mark Feng Teng

Data-Driven Learning In and Out of the Language Classroom
Pascual Pérez-Paredes and Alex Boulton

Language Teacher Emotions
Juyoung Song and Elizabeth R. Miller

A full series listing is available at: www.cambridge.org/ELAT

Printed by Libri Plureos GmbH in Hamburg, Germany